BUSINESS IS A WAR STRATEGIZE ABOUT HOW TO WIN THE BATTLE

ARVIND UPADHYAY

Our research confirms that there are no permanently excellent companies, just as there are no permanently excellent industries. As we have found on our own tumbling road, we all, like corporations, do smart things and less-than-smart things. To improve the quality of our success we need to study what we did that made a positive difference and understand how to replicate it systematically. That is what we call making smart strategic moves, and we have found that the strategic move that matters centrally is to create blue oceans.

In 1805, England had a problem. Napoléon had conquered big chunks of Europe and planned the invasion of England. But to cross the Channel, he needed to wrest control of the sea away from the English. Off the southwest coast of Spain, the French and Spanish combined fleet of thirty-three ships met the smaller British fleet of twenty-seven ships. The well-developed tactics of the day were for the two opposing fleets to each stay in line, firing broadsides at each other. But British admiral Lord Nelson had a strategic insight. He broke the British fleet into two columns and drove them at the Franco-Spanish fleet, hitting their line perpendicularly. The lead British ships took a great risk, but Nelson judged that the less-trained Franco-Spanish gunners would not be able to compensate for the heavy swell that day. At the end of the Battle of Trafalgar, the French and Spanish lost twenty-two ships, two-thirds of their fleet. The British lost none. Nelson was mortally wounded, becoming, in death, Britain's greatest naval hero. Britain's naval dominance was ensured and remained unsurpassed for a century and a half. Nelson's challenge was that he was outnumbered. His strategy was to risk his lead ships in order to break the coherence of his enemy's fleet. With coherence lost, he judged, the more experienced English captains would come out on top in the ensuing melee. Good strategy almost always looks this simple and obvious and does not take a thick deck of PowerPoint slides to explain. It does not pop out of some "strategic management" tool, matrix, chart, triangle, or fill-in-the-blanks scheme. Instead, a talented leader identifies the one or two critical issues in the situation—the pivot points that can multiply the effectiveness of effort—and then focuses and concentrates action and resources on them. Despite the roar of voices wanting to equate strategy with ambition, leadership, "vision," planning, or the economic logic of competition, strategy is none of these. The core of strategy work is always the same: discovering the critical factors in a situation and designing a way of coordinating and focusing actions to deal with those factors. A leader's most important responsibility is identifying the biggest challenges to forward progress and devising a coherent approach to overcoming them. In contexts ranging from corporate direction to national security, strategy matters. Yet we have become so accustomed to strategy as exhortation that we hardly blink an eye when a leader spouts slogans and announces high-sounding goals, calling the mixture a "strategy." Here are four examples of this syndrome. • The event was a "strategy retreat." The CEO had modeled it on a similar event at British Airways he had attended several years before. About two hundred upper-level managers from around the world gathered in a hotel ballroom where top management presented a vision for the future: to be the most respected and successful company in their field. There was a specially produced motion picture featuring the firm's products and services being used in colorful settings around the world. There was an address by the CEO accompanied by dramatic music to highlight the company's "strategic" goals: global leadership, growth, and high shareholder return. There were breakouts into smaller groups to allow discussion and buy-in. There was a colorful release of balloons. There was everything but strategy. A specialist in bonds, Lehman Brothers had been a pioneer in the new wave of mortgagebacked securities that buoyed Wall Street in the 2002–6 period. By 2006, signs of strain were appearing: U.S. home sales had peaked in mid-2005, and home price appreciation had stopped. A small increase in the Fed's interest rate had triggered an increase in foreclosures. Lehman CEO Richard Fuld's response, formalized in 2006, was a "strategy" of continuing to gain market share by growing faster than the rest of the industry. In the language of Wall Street, Lehman would do this by increasing its "risk appetite." That is, it would take on the deals its competitors were rejecting. Operating with only 3 percent equity, and much of its debt supplied on a very short-term basis, this policy should have been accompanied by clever ways of mitigating the increased risk. A good strategy recognizes the nature of the challenge and offers a way of surmounting it. Simply being ambitious is not a strategy. In 2008, Lehman Brothers ended its 158 years as an investment bank with a crash that sent the global financial system into a tailspin. Here, the consequences of bad strategy were disastrous for Lehman, the United States, and the world.In 2003, President George W. Bush authorized the U.S. military to invade and conquer Iraq. The invasion went quickly. Once the army-to-army fighting stopped, administration leaders had expected to oversee a rapid transition to a democratic civil society in Iraq. Instead, as a violent insurgency gathered momentum, individual units of the U.S. military fell back on running "search and destroy" missions out of secure bases—the same approach that had failed so badly in Vietnam. There were numerous high-sounding goals—freedom, democracy, reconstruction, security—but no coherent strategy for dealing with the insurgency. The change came in 2007. Having just written the Army/Marine Corps Counterinsurgency Field Manual, General David Petraeus was sent to Iraq, along with five additional brigades of troops. But more than the extra soldiers, Petraeus was armed with an actual strategy. His idea was that one could combat an insurgency as long as the large preponderance of civilians supported a legitimate government. The trick was to shift the military's focus from making patrols to protecting the populace. A populace that was not in fear of insurgent retaliation would provide the information necessary to isolate and combat the insurgent minority. This change, replacing amorphous goals with a true problem-solving strategy, made an enormous difference in the results achieved.he key insight driving this book is the hard-won lesson of a lifetime of experience at strategy work—as a consultant to organizations, as a personal adviser, as a teacher, and as a researcher. A good strategy does more than urge us forward toward a goal or vision. A good strategy honestly acknowledges the challenges being faced and provides an approach to overcoming them. And the greater the challenge, the more a good strategy focuses and coordinates efforts to achieve a powerful competitive punch or problem-solving effect. Unfortunately, good strategy is the exception, not the rule. And the problem is growing. More and more organizational leaders say they have a strategy, but they do not. Instead, they espouse what I call bad strategy. Bad strategy tends to skip over pesky details such as problems. It ignores the power of choice and focus, trying instead to accommodate a multitude of conflicting demands and interests. Like a quarterback whose only advice to teammates is "Let's win," bad strategy covers up its failure to guide by embracing the language of broad goals, ambition, vision, and values. Each of these elements is, of course, an important part of human life. But, by themselves, they are not substitutes for the hard work of strategy

Execution of blue ocean strategy as systematic and actionable as competing in the red waters of known market space. Only then can companies step up to the challenge of creating blue oceans in a smart and responsible way that is both opportunity maximizing and risk minimizing. No company—large or small, incumbent or new entrant—can afford to be a riverboat gambler. And no company should. The contents of this book are based on more than fifteen years of research, data stretching back more than a hundred years, and a series of Harvard Business Review articles as well as academic articles on various dimensions of this topic. The ideas, tools, and frameworks presented here have been further tested and refined over the years in corporate practice in Europe, the United States, and Asia. This book builds on and extends this work by providing a narrative arc that draws these ideas together to offer a unified framework. This framework addresses not only the analytic aspects behind the creation of blue ocean strategy but also the allimportant human aspects of how to bring an organization and its people on this journey with a willingness to execute these ideas in action. Here, understanding how to build trust and commitment, as well as an understanding of the importance of intellectual and emotional recognition, are highlighted and brought to the core of strategy. Blue ocean opportunities have been out there. As they have been explored, the market universe has been expanding. This expansion, we believe, is the root of growth. Yet poor understanding exists both in theory and in practice as to how to systematically create and capture blue oceans. We invite you to read this book to learn how you can be a driver of this expansion in the future.

A word that can mean anything has lost its bite. To give content to a concept one has to draw lines, marking off what it denotes and what it does not. To begin the journey toward clarity, it is helpful to recognize that the words "strategy" and "strategic" are often sloppily used to mark decisions made by the highest-level officials. For example, in business, most mergers and acquisitions, investments in expensive new facilities, negotiations with important suppliers and customers, and overall organizational design are normally considered to be "strategic." However, when you speak of "strategy," you should not be simply marking the pay grade of the decision maker. Rather, the term "strategy" should mean a cohesive response to an important challenge. Unlike a stand-alone decision or a goal, a strategy is a coherent set of analyses, concepts, policies, arguments, and actions that respond to a high-stakes challenge. Many people assume that a strategy is a big-picture overall direction, divorced from any specific action. But defining strategy as broad concepts, thereby leaving out action, creates a wide chasm between "strategy" and "implementation." If you accept this chasm, most strategy work becomes wheel spinning. Indeed, this is the most common complaint about "strategy." Echoing many others, one top executive told me, "We have a sophisticated strategy process, but there is a huge problem of execution. We almost always fall short of the goals we set for ourselves." If you have followed my line of argument, you can see the reason for this complaint. A good strategy includes a set of coherent actions. They are not "implementation" details; they are the punch in the strategy. A strategy that fails to define a variety of plausible and feasible immediate actions is missing a critical component. Executives who complain about "execution" problems have usually confused strategy with goal setting. When the "strategy" process is basically a game of setting performance goals—so much market share and so much profit, so many students graduating high school, so many visitors to the museum—then there remains a yawning gap between these ambitions and action. Strategy is about how an organization will move forward. Doing strategy is figuring out how to advance the organization's interests. Of course, a leader can set goals and delegate to others the job of figuring out what to do. But that is not strategy. If that is how the organization runs, let's skip the spin and be honest—call it goal setting.

Contents

CHAPTER ONE

GOOD AND BAD STRATEGY

The most basic idea of strategy is the application of strength against weakness. Or, if you prefer, strength applied to the most promising opportunity. The standard modern treatment of strategy has expanded this idea into a rich discussion of potential strengths, today called "advantages." There are advantages due to being a first mover: scale, scope, network effects, reputation, patents, brands, and hundreds more. None of these are logically wrong, and each can be important. Yet this whole midlevel framework misses two huge, incredibly important natural sources of strength: 1. Having a coherent strategy—one that coordinates policies and actions. A good strategy doesn't just draw on existing strength; it creates strength through the coherence of its design. Most organizations of any size don't do this. Rather, they pursue multiple objectives that are unconnected with one another or, worse, that conflict with one another. 2. The creation of new strengths through subtle shifts in viewpoint. An insightful reframing of a competitive situation can create whole new patterns of advantage and weakness. The most powerful strategies arise from such game-changing insights.

The leader of an organization lacking a good strategy may simply believe that strategy is unnecessary. But more often the lack is due to the presence of bad strategy. Like weeds crowding out the grass, bad strategy crowds out good strategy. Leaders using bad strategies have not just chosen the wrong goals or made implementation errors. Rather, they have mistaken views about what strategy is and how it works.

GOOD STRATEGY IS UNEXPECTED

The first natural advantage of good strategy arises because other organizations often don't have one. And because they don't expect you to have one, either. A good strategy has coherence, coordinating actions, policies, and resources so as to accomplish an important end. Many organizations, most of the time, don't have this. Instead, they have multiple goals and initiatives that symbolize progress, but no coherent approach to accomplishing that progress other than "spend more and try harder." APPLE After the 1995 release of Microsoft's Windows 95 multimedia operating system, Apple Inc. fell into a death spiral. On February 5, 1996, BusinessWeek put Apple's famous trademark on its cover to illustrate its lead story: "The Fall of an American Icon." CEO Gil Amelio struggled to keep Apple alive in a world being rapidly dominated by WindowsIntel-based PCs. He cut staff. He reorganized the company's many products into four groups: Macintosh, information appliances, printers and peripherals, and "alternative platforms." A new Internet Services Group was added to the Operating Systems Group and the Advanced Technology Group. Wired magazine carried an article titled "101 Ways to Save Apple." It included suggestions such as "Sell yourself to IBM or Motorola," "Invest heavily in Newton technology," and "Exploit your advantage in the K–12 education market." Wall Street analysts hoped for and urged a deal with Sony or Hewlett-Packard. By September 1997, Apple was two months from bankruptcy. Steve Jobs, who had cofounded the company in 1976, agreed to return to serve on a reconstructed board of directors and to be interim CEO. Die-hard fans of the original Macintosh were overjoyed, but the general business world was not expecting much. Within a year, things changed radically at Apple. Although many observers had expected Jobs to rev up the development of advanced products, or engineer a deal with Sun, he did neither. What he did was both obvious and, at the same time, unexpected. He shrunk Apple to a scale and scope suitable to the reality of its being a niche producer in the highly competitive personal computer business. He cut Apple back to a core that could survive. Steve Jobs talked Microsoft into investing $150 million in Apple, exploiting Bill Gates's concerns about what a failed Apple would mean to Microsoft's struggle with the Department of Justice. Jobs cut all of the desktop models—there were fifteen—back to one. He cut all portable and handheld models back to one laptop. He completely cut out all the printers and other peripherals. He cut development engineers. He cut software development. He cut distributors and cut out five of the company's six national retailers. He cut out virtually all manufacturing, moving it offshore to Taiwan. With a simpler product line manufactured in Asia, he cut inventory by more than 80 percent. A new

Web store sold Apple's products directly to consumers, cutting out distributors and dealers. What is remarkable about Jobs's turnaround strategy for Apple is how much it was "BusinBusiness 101 is surprisingess 101" and yet how much of it was unanticipated. Of course you have to cut back and simplify to your core to climb out of a financial nosedive. Of course he needed up-to-date versions of Microsoft's Office software to work on Apple's computers. Of course Dell's model of Asian supply-chain manufacturing, short cycle times, and negative working capital was the state of the art in the industry and deserved emulation. Of course he stopped the development of new operating systems—he had just brought the industry's best operating system with him from NeXT. The power of Jobs's strategy came from directly tackling the fundamental problem with a focused and coordinated set of actions. He did not announce ambitious revenue or profit goals; he did not indulge in messianic visions of the future. And he did not just cut in a blind ax-wielding frenzy—he redesigned the whole business logic around a simplified product line sold through a limited set of outlets. In May 1998, while trying to help strike a deal between Apple and Telecom Italia, I had the chance to talk to Jobs about his approach to turning Apple around. He explained both the substance and coherence of his insight with a few sentences: The product lineup was too complicated and the company was bleeding cash. A friend of the family asked me which Apple computer she should buy. She couldn't figure out the differences among them and I couldn't give her clear guidance, either. I was appalled that there was no Apple consumer computer priced under $2,000. We are replacing all of those desktop computers with one, the Power Mac G3. We are dropping five of six national retailers—meeting their demand has meant too many models at too many price points and too much markup. This kind of focused action is far from the norm in industry. Eighteen months earlier, I had been involved in a large-scale study, sponsored by Andersen Consulting, of strategies in the worldwide electronics industry. Working in Europe, I carried out interviews with twenty-six executives, all division managers or CEOs in the electronics and telecommunications sector. My interview plan was simple: I asked each executive to identify the leading competitor in their business. I asked how that company had become the leader—evoking their private theories about what works. And then I asked them what their own company's current strategy was. These executives, by and large, had no trouble describing the strategy of the leader in their sectors. The standard story was that some change in demand or technology had appeared—a "window of opportunity" had opened—and the current leader had been the first one to leap through that window and take advantage of it. Not necessarily the first mover, but the first to get it right. But when I asked about their own companies' strategies, there was a very different kind of response. Instead of pointing to the next window of opportunity, or even mentioning its possibility, I heard a lot of look-busy doorknob polishing. They were making alliances, they were doing 360-degree feedback, they were looking for foreign markets, they were setting challenging strategic goals, they were moving software into firmware, they were enabling Internet updates of firmware, and so on. They had each told me the formula for success in the 1990s electronics industry—take a good position quickly when a new window of opportunity opens—but none said that was their focus or even mentioned it as part of their strategy. Given that background, I was interested in what Steve Jobs might say about the future of Apple. His survival strategy for Apple, for all its skill and drama, was not going to propel Apple into the future. At that moment in time, Apple had less than 4 percent of the personal computer market. The de facto standard was Windows-Intel and there seemed to be no way for Apple to do more than just hang on to a tiny niche. In the summer of 1998, I got an opportunity to talk with Jobs again. I said, "Steve, this turnaround at Apple has been impressive. But everything we know about the PC business says that Apple cannot really push beyond a small niche position. The network effects are just too strong to upset the Wintel standard. So what are you trying to do in the longer term? What is the strategy?" He did not attack my argument. He didn't agree with it, either. He just smiled and said, "I am going to wait for the next big thing." Jobs did not enunciate some simple-minded growth or market share goal. He did not pretend that pushing on various levers would somehow magically restore Apple to market leadership in personal computers. Instead, he was actually focused on the sources of and barriers to success in his industry —recognizing the next window of opportunity, the next set of forces he could harness to his advantage, and then having the quickness and cleverness to pounce on it quickly like a perfect predator. There was no pretense that such windows opened every year or that one could force them open with incentives or management tricks. He knew how it worked. He had done it before with the Apple II and the Macintosh and then with Pixar. He had tried to force it with NeXT, and that had not gone well. It would be two years before he would make that leap again with the iPod and then online music. And, after that, with the iPhone. Steve Jobs's answer that day—"to wait for the next big thing"—is not a general formula for success. But it was a wise approach to Apple's situation at that moment, in that industry, with so many new technologies seemingly just around the corner. DESERT STORM Another example of surprise at the existence of a strategy occurred at the end of the first Gulf War in 1991. People were surprised to discover that U.S. commanders actually had a focused strategy for defeating the entrenched Iraqi invaders. On August 2, 1990, Iraq invaded Kuwait. Led by elite troops making airborne and amphibious landings, and four divisions of the Republican Guard, 150,000 Iraqi soldiers rolled into and occupied Kuwait. It is probable that Saddam Hussein's primary motive for the invasion was financial. The eight-year war he had started by invading Iran in 1980 had left his regime with massive debts to Kuwait and other Gulf states. By taking Kuwait and declaring it the nineteenth province of Iraq, Saddam would cancel his debts to that country and be able to use its massive oil income to repay his debts to other nations. Five months later, a thirty-three-nation coalition organized by U.S. president George H. W. Bush was carrying out air strikes against Iraqi forces and rapidly building its ground forces. Iraq, in turn, had increased its force in Kuwait to more than five hundred thousand. It was hoped that air power alone might produce a resolution of the conflict, but if it did not, a ground offensive would be necessary to reverse Iraq's invasion and occupation of Kuwait. There was no real doubt that the coalition had the ability to throw back the Iraqis. But how costly would it be? In October 1990, the French newspaper L'Express had estimated that retaking Kuwait would take about a week and cost twenty thousand U.S. casualties. As Iraqi forces swelled and built defensive positions, public discussion in the press, on television, and in the halls of Congress began to evoke images of World War I trench combat. In Congress, Senator Bob Graham (D-Florida) noted that "Iraq already has had five months to dig in and to fortify and they have done so in a major way. Kuwait has fortifications reminiscent of World War I." In the same vein, the New York Times described a battalion of the Sixteenth Infantry as "the men who expect to have the job of slogging it out in the trenches of Kuwait with their M-16 rifles and M-60 machine guns blazing." Time magazine described the Iraqi defenses this way: In an area about the size of West Virginia the Iraqis have poured 540,000 of their millionman army and 4,000 of their 6,000 tanks, along with thousands of other armored vehicles and artillery pieces.... Iraqi units are entrenched in their now traditional triangular forts, formed of packed sand, with an infantry company equipped with heavy machine guns holding each corner. Soldiers are protected by portable concrete shelters or dugouts of sheet metal and sand. Tanks are hull deep in the ground and bolstered with sandbags. Artillery pieces are deployed at the apex of each triangle, pre-aimed at "killing zones" created by flaming trenches and minefields. 1 On the eve of the ground assault, the Los Angeles Times reminded its readers that "Iraqi troops along the front lines are well dug in, and assaulting such fortified positions is always a risky business. The debacles at Cold Harbor, the Somme and Gallipoli are grim reminders of the price of failure. Even success, as at Tarawa, Okinawa or Hamburger Hill, can come at a terrible price." 2 What these commentators did not predict was that General Norman Schwarzkopf, commander in chief of U.S. Central Command, had a strategy for the ground war, a strategy he had developed back in early October. The original plan generated by his staff, a direct attack into Kuwait, was estimated to cost 2,000 dead and 8,000 wounded. Schwarzkopf rejected this approach in favor of a two-pronged plan. Air attacks would be used to reduce the Iraqi capabilities by 50 percent. Then he planned a massive secret "left hook." While the world's attention was focused on CNN's 24/7 coverage of troops just south of Kuwait, the coalition would secretly shift a force of 250,000 soldiers well west of Kuwait and then have them move north into positions in the empty desert of southern Iraq. When the ground war began, this force would continue north and then turn east, completing the "left hook," and slamming into the flank of the Iraqi Republican Guard. Attacks aimed northward into Kuwait itself were to be minor. The U.S. Marines ground forces were ordered to move slowly northward into Kuwait, a ploy to entice the entrenched Iraqis southward and out of their fortifications, where they would be hit from the side by part of the massive left hook. The sea-based marines would not land, their floating presence being a diversion. Schwarzkopf's combined-arms left-hook strategy was so successful that the intense ground war lasted only one hundred hours. A month of air bombardment had conditioned Iraqi troops to disperse and hide their tanks and artillery, stay out of their vehicles, and keep motors off. The swiftness and violence of the coalition ground assault, combining tanks, infantry, attack helicopters, and bombers, was decisive. Republican Guard units fought bravely but were unable to maneuver or call in reserves fast enough to respond to the speed and ferocity of the attack. Finally, and perhaps most important, Saddam Hussein had ordered his commanders not to use their chemical weapons. These artillery shells, used to halt Iranian attacks during the Iran-Iraq War, would have caused thousands of coalition casualties. Marine commanders had estimated they would lose 20 to 30 percent of their force if chemical weapons were used against them. 3 But Saddam was deterred—postwar intelligence gleaned from the Russians revealed that he feared a U.S. nuclear retaliation to such use. Iraq fled Kuwait, much of its invading army destroyed. 4 Coalition casualties were light—on the first day there were eight dead and twenty-seven wounded. The coalition's success with the combined-arms left-hook strategy was so stark that pundits who were worried about trench warfare in February were, by March, opining that the coalition had amassed more forces than it needed and that the outcome had been a foregone conclusion. Schwarzkopf revealed the ground-war strategy to the public in a widely viewed press briefing. Most people who saw this briefing and the map of the left hook were surprised and impressed. News commentators described the plan as "brilliant" and "secret." Few had anticipated this envelopment maneuver. But why hadn't they? The Department of the Army publishes field manuals fully describing its basic doctrines and methods. FM 100-5, published in 1986, was titled Operations and was described as "the Army's keystone warfighting manual."

Envelopment avoids the enemy's front, where its forces are most protected and his fires most easily concentrated. Instead, while fixing the defender's attention forward by supporting or diversionary attacks, the attacker maneuvers his main effort around or over the enemy's defenses to strike at his flanks and rear. To illustrate this maneuver, FM 100-5 Operations offered a diagram reproduced on the facing page. Given this vivid picture of a feint up the middle combined with a powerful "left hook," one must ask: "How could Schwarzkopf's use of the primary of ensive doctrine of the U.S. Army have been a surprise to anyone?" Some part of the answer lies in successful deception. Schwarzkopf intended to make it appear that the main attack would be launched into Kuwait from the sea and then overland directly into Iraqi defenses. This was supported by an early visible amphibious raid on the Kuwaiti coast and by actions to destroy Iraq's navy. The press unwittingly helped in this misdirection by reporting on the photogenic amphibious training, the build-up of troops just south of Kuwait, and then by anguishing over the prospect of World War I trench warfare. But an essential element of the U.S. Army's "Plan A"—envelopment—is the illusion of a direct attack coupled with a much more massive end run. And, since "Plan A" was available to anyone with twenty-five dollars to send to the U.S. Government Printing Office, 5 it remains puzzling as to why "Plan A" was a surprise—a surprise not only to Iraq but also to talking-head military commentators on television and to most of the U.S. Congress. The best answer to this puzzle is that the real surprise was that such a pure and focused strategy was actually implemented. Most complex organizations spread rather than concentrate resources, acting to placate and pay off internal and external interests. Thus, we are surprised when a complex organization, such as Apple or the U.S. Army, actually focuses its actions. Not because of secrecy, but because good strategy itself is unexpected. In the case of Desert Storm, the focus was much more than an intellectual step. Schwarzkopf had to suppress the ambitions and desires of the air force, marines, various army units, each coalition partner, and the political leadership in Washington. For example, the U.S. Army's best light infantry— the Eighty-Second Airborne—was tasked with providing support to French armor and infantry, an assignment its leadership protested. Eight thousand U.S. Marines waited on ships to land on the beaches of Kuwait City, but did not. It was a diversion. Air force commanders wanted to demonstrate the value of strategic bombing—they believed that the war could be won by air attacks on Baghdad— and had to be forced against strenuous protest to divert their resources to fully support the land offensive. Secretary of Defense Dick Cheney wanted the mission accomplished with a smaller force and detailed an alternative plan of attack. Prince Khalid, commanding the Saudi forces in the coalition, insisted that King Fahd be involved in the planning, but Schwarzkopf convinced President Bush to ensure that U.S. Central Command retained control over strategy and planning. ENVELOPMENT Having conflicting goals, dedicating resources to unconnected targets, and accommodating incompatible interests are the luxuries of the rich and powerful, but they make for bad strategy. Despite this, most organizations will not create focused strategies. Instead, they will generate laundry lists of desirable outcomes and, at the same time, ignore the need for genuine competence in coordinating and focusing their resources. Good strategy requires leaders who are willing and able to say no to a wide variety of actions and interests. Strategy is at least as much about what an organization does not do as it is about what it does.

CHAPTER TWO

Creating Blue Oceans

AONE TIME ACCORDION PLAYER, stilt-walker, and fireeater, Guy Laliberté is now CEO of Cirque du Soleil, one of Canada's largest cultural exports. Created in 1984 by a group of street performers, Cirque's productions have been seen by almost forty million people in ninety cities around the world. In less than twenty years Cirque du Soleil has achieved a level of revenues that took Ringling Bros. and Barnum & Bailey—the global champion of the circus industry—more than one hundred years to attain. What makes this rapid growth all the more remarkable is that it was not achieved in an attractive industry but rather in a declining industry in which traditional strategic analysis pointed to limited potential for growth. Supplier power on the part of star performers was strong. So was buyer power. Alternative forms of entertainment—ranging from various kinds of urban live entertainment to sporting events to home entertainment—cast an increasingly long shadow. Children cried out for PlayStations rather than a visit to the traveling circus. Partially as a result, the industry was suffering from steadily decreasing audiences and, in turn, declining revenue and profits. There was also increasing sentiment against the use of animals in circuses by animal rights groups. Ringling Bros. and Barnum & Bailey set the standard, and competing smaller circuses essentially followed with scaled-down versions. From the perspective of competition-based strategy, then, the circus industry appeared unattractive. Another compelling aspect of Cirque du Soleil's success is that it did not win by taking customers from the already shrinking circus industry, which historically catered to children. Cirque du Soleil did not compete with Ringling Bros. and Barnum & Bailey. Instead it created uncontested new market space that made the competition irrelevant. It appealed to a whole new group of customers: adults and corporate clients prepared to pay a price several times as great as traditional circuses for an unprecedented entertainment experience.

Significantly, one of the first Cirque productions was titled "We Reinvent the Circus." New Market Space Cirque du Soleil succeeded because it realized that to win in the future, companies must stop competing with each other. The only way to beat the competition is to stop trying to beat the competition. To understand what Cirque du Soleil has achieved, imagine a market universe composed of two sorts of oceans: red oceans and blue oceans. Red oceans represent all the industries in existence today. This is the known market space. Blue oceans denote all the industries not in existence today. This is the unknown market space. In the red oceans, industry boundaries are defined and accepted, and the competitive rules of the game are known.1 Here, companies try to outperform their rivals to grab a greater share of existing demand. As the market space gets crowded, prospects for profits and growth are reduced. Products become commodities, and cutthroat competition turns the red ocean bloody. Blue oceans, in contrast, are defined by untapped market space, demand creation, and the opportunity for highly profitable growth.

Although some blue oceans are created well beyond existing industry boundaries, most are created from within red oceans by expanding existing industry boundaries, as Cirque du Soleil did. In blue oceans, competition is irrelevant because the rules of the game are waiting to be set. It will always be important to swim successfully in the red ocean by outcompeting rivals. Red oceans will always matter and will always be a fact of business life. But with supply exceeding demand in more industries, competing for a share of contracting markets, while necessary, will not be sufficient to sustain high performance.2 Companies need to go beyond competing. To seize new profit and growth opportunities, they also need to create blue oceans. Unfortunately, blue oceans are largely uncharted. The dominant focus of strategy work over the past twenty-five years has been on competition-based red ocean strategies.3 The result has been a fairly good understanding of how to compete skillfully in red waters, from analyzing the underlying economic structure of an existing industry, to choosing a strategic position of low cost or differentiation or focus, to benchmarking the competition. Some discussions around blue oceans exist.4 However, there is little practical guidance on how to create them. Without analytic frameworks to create blue oceans and principles to effectively manage risk, creating blue oceans has remained wishful thinking that is seen as too risky for managers to pursue as strategy. This book provides practical frameworks and analytics for the systematic pursuit and capture of blue oceans. The

Continuing Creation of Blue Oceans Although the term blue oceans is new, their existence is not. They are a feature of business life, past and present. Look back one hundred years and ask yourself, How many of today's industries were then unknown? The answer: Many industries as basic as automobiles, music recording, aviation, petrochemicals, health care, and management consulting were unheard of or had just begun to emerge at that time. Now turn the clock back only thirty years. Again, a plethora of multibillion-dollar industries jumps out—mutual funds, cell phones, gas-fired electricity plants, biotechnology, discount retail, express package delivery, minivans, snowboards, coffee bars, and home videos, to name a few. Just three decades ago, none of these industries existed in a meaningful way. Now put the clock forward twenty years—or perhaps fifty years— and ask yourself how many now unknown industries will likely exist then. If history is any predictor of the future, again the answer is many of them. The reality is that industries never stand still. They continuously evolve. Operations improve, markets expand, and players come and go. History teaches us that we have a hugely underestimated capacity to create new industries and re-create existing ones. In fact, the half-century-old Standard Industrial Classification (SIC) system published by the U.S. Census was replaced in 1997 by the North America Industry Classification Standard (NAICS) system. The new system expanded the ten SIC industry sectors into twenty sectors to reflect the emerging realities of new industry territories.5 The services sector under the old system, for example, is now expanded into seven business sectors ranging from information to health care and social assistance.6 Given that these systems are designed for standardization and continuity, such a replacement shows how significant the expansion of blue oceans has been. Yet the overriding focus of strategic thinking has been on competition-based red ocean strategies. Part of the explanation for this is that corporate strategy is heavily influenced by its roots in military strategy. The very language of strategy is deeply imbued with military references—chief executive "officers" in "headquarters," "troops" on the "front lines." Described this way, strategy is about confronting an opponent and fighting over a given piece of land that is both limited and constant.7 Unlike war, however, the history of industry shows us that the market universe has never been constant; rather, blue oceans have continuously been created over time. To focus on the red ocean is therefore to accept the key constraining factors of war—limited terrain and the need to beat an enemy to succeed—and to deny the distinctive strength of the business world: the capacity to create new market space that is uncontested. The Impact of Creating Blue Oceans We set out to quantify the impact of creating blue oceans on a company's growth in both revenues and profits in a study of the business launches of 108 companies (see figure 1-1). We found that 86 percent of the launches were line extensions, that is, incremental improvements within the red ocean of existing market space. Yet they accounted for only 62 percent of total revenues and a mere 39 percent of total profits. The remaining 14 percent of the launches were aimed at creating blue oceans. They generated 38 percent of total revenues and 61 percent of total profits. Given that business launches included the total investments made for creating red and blue oceans (regardless of their subsequent revenue and profit consequences, including failures), the performance benefits of creating blue waters are evident. Although we don't have data on the hit rate of success of red and blue ocean initiatives, the global performance differences between them are marked. The Rising Imperative of Creating Blue Oceans There are several driving forces behind a rising imperative to create blue oceans. Accelerated technological advances have substantially improved industrial productivity and have allowed suppliers to produce an unprecedented array of products and services. The result is that in increasing numbers of industries, supply exceeds demand.8 The trend toward globalization compounds the situation. As trade barriers between nations and regions are dismantled and as information on products and prices becomes instantly and globally available, niche markets and havens for monopoly continue to disappear.9 While supply is on the rise as global competition intensifies, there is no clear evidence of an increase in demand worldwide, and statistics even point to declining populations in many developed markets.10 The result has been accelerated commoditization of products and services, increasing price wars, and shrinking profit margins. Recent industrywide studies on major American brands confirm this trend.11 They reveal that for major product and service categories, brands are generally becoming more similar, and as they are becoming more similar people increasingly select based on price.12 People no longer insist, as in the past, that their laundry detergent be Tide. Nor will they necessarily stick to Colgate when Crest is on sale, and vice versa. In overcrowded industries, differentiating brands becomes harder in both economic upturns and downturns. All this suggests that the business environment in which most strategy and management approaches of the twentieth century evolved is increasingly disappearing. As red oceans become increasingly bloody, management will need to be more concerned with blue oceans than the current cohort of managers is accustomed to.From Company and Industry to Strategic Move How can a company break out of the red ocean of bloody competition? How can it create a blue ocean? Is there a systematic approach to achieve this and thereby sustain high performance? In search of an answer, our initial step was to define the basic unit of analysis for our research. To understand the roots of high performance, the business literature typically uses the company as the basic unit of analysis. People have marveled at how companies attain strong, profitable growth with a distinguished set of strategic, operational, and organizational characteristics. Our question, however, was this: Are there lasting "excellent" or "visionary" companies that continuously outperform the market and repeatedly create blue oceans? Consider, for example, In Search of Excellence and Built to Last. 13 The bestselling book In Search of Excellence was published twenty years ago. Yet within two years of its publication a number of the companies surveyed began to slip into oblivion: Atari, ChesebroughPond's, Data General, Fluor, National Semiconductor. As documented in Managing on the Edge, two-thirds of the identified model firms in the book had fallen from their perches as industry leaders within five years of its publication.14 The book Built to Last continued in the same footsteps. It sought out the "successful habits of visionary companies" that had a longrunning track record of superior performance. To avoid the pitfalls of In Search of Excellence, however, the survey period of Built to Last was expanded to the entire life span of the companies while its analysis was limited to firms more than forty years old. Built to Last also became a bestseller. But again, upon closer examination, deficiencies in some of the visionary companies spotlighted in Built to Last have come to light. As illustrated in the recent book Creative Destruction, much of the success attributed to some of the model companies in Built to Last was the result of industry sector performance rather than the companies themselves.15 For example, Hewlett-Packard (HP) met the criteria of Built to Last by outperforming the market over the long term. In reality, while HP outperformed the market, so did the entire computer-hardware industry. What's more, HP did not even outperform the competition within the industry. Through this and other examples, Creative Destruction questioned whether "visionary" companies that continuously outperform the market have ever existed. And we all have seen the stagnating or declining performance of the Japanese companies that were celebrated as "revolutionary" strategists in their heyday of the late 1970s and early 1980s. If there is no perpetually high-performing company and if the same company can be brilliant at one moment and wrongheaded at another, it appears that the company is not the appropriate unit of analysis in exploring the roots of high performance and blue oceans. As discussed earlier, history also shows that industries are constantly being created and expanded over time and that industry conditions and boundaries are not given; individual actors can shape them. Companies need not compete head-on in a given industry space; Cirque du Soleil created a new market space in the entertainment sector, generating strong, profitable growth as a result. It appears, then, that neither the company nor the industry is the best unit of analysis in studying the roots of profitable growth. Consistent with this observation, our study shows that the strategic move, and not the company or the industry, is the right unit of analysis for explaining the creation of blue oceans and sustained high performance. A strategic move is the set of managerial actions and decisions involved in making a major market-creating business offering. Compaq, for example, was acquired by HewlettPackard in 2001 and ceased to be an independent company. As a result, many people might judge the company as unsuccessful. This does not, however, invalidate the blue ocean strategic moves that Compaq made in creating the server industry. These strategic moves not only were a part of the company's powerful comeback in the mid-1990s but also unlocked a new multibillion-dollar market space in computing ."A Sketch of the Historical Pattern of Blue Ocean Creation," provides a snapshot overview of the history of three representative U.S. industries drawn from our database: the auto industry—how we get to work; the computer industry—what we use at work; and the cinema industry—where we go after work for enjoyment. As shown in appendix A, no perpetually excellent company or industry is found. But a striking commonality appears to exist across strategic moves that have created blue oceans and have led to new trajectories of strong, profitable growth. The strategic moves we discuss—moves that have delivered products and services that opened and captured new market space, with a significant leap in demand—contain great stories of profitable growth as well as thought-provoking tales of missed opportunities by companies stuck in red oceans. We built our study around these strategic moves to understand the pattern by which blue oceans are created and high performance achieved. We studied more than one hundred fifty strategic moves made from 1880 to 2000 in more than thirty industries, and we closely examined the relevant business players in each of these events. Industries ranged from hotels, the cinema, retail, airlines, energy, computers, broadcasting, and construction to automobiles and steel. We analyzed not only winning business players who created blue oceans but also their less successful competitors. Both within a given strategic move and across strategic moves, we searched for convergence among the group that created blue oceans and within less successful players caught in the red ocean. We also searched for divergence across these two groups. In so doing, we tried to discover the common factors leading to the creation of blue oceans and the key differences separating those winners from the mere survivors and the losers adrift in the red ocean. Our analysis of more than thirty industries confirms that neither industry nor organizational characteristics explain the distinction between the two groups. In assessing industry, organizational, and strategic variables we found that the creation and capturing of blue oceans were achieved by small and large companies, by young and old managers, by companies in attractive and unattractive industries, by new entrants and established incumbents, by private and public companies, by companies in low- and high-tech industries, and by companies of diverse national origins. Our analysis failed to find any perpetually excellent company or industry. What we did find behind the seemingly idiosyncratic success stories, however, was a consistent and common pattern across strategic moves for creating and capturing blue oceans. Whether it was Ford in 1908 with the Model T; GM in 1924 with cars styled to appeal to the emotions; CNN in 1980 with real-time news 24/7; or Compaq, Starbucks, Southwest Airlines, or Cirque du Soleil—or, for that matter, any of the other blue ocean moves in our study—the approach to strategy in creating blue oceans was consistent across time regardless of industry. Our research also reached out to embrace famous strategic moves in public sector turnarounds. Here we found a strikingly similar pattern. Value Innovation: The Cornerstone of Blue Ocean Strategy What consistently separated winners from losers in creating blue oceans was their approach to strategy. The companies caught in the red ocean followed a conventional approach, racing to beat the competition by building a defensible position within the existing industry order.16 The creators of blue oceans, surprisingly, didn't use the competition as their benchmark.17 Instead, they followed a different strategic logic that we call value innovation. Value innovation is the cornerstone of blue ocean strategy. We call it value innovation because instead of focusing on beating the competition, you focus on making the competition irrelevant by creating a leap in value for buyers and your company, thereby opening up new and uncontested market space. Value innovation places equal emphasis on value and innovation. Value without innovation tends to focus on value creation onan incremental scale, something that improves value but is not sufficient to make you stand out in the marketplace.18 Innovation without value tends to be technology-driven, market pioneering, or futuristic, often shooting beyond what buyers are ready to accept and pay for.19 In this sense, it is important to distinguish between value innovation as opposed to technology innovation and market pioneering. Our study shows that what separates winners from losers in creating blue oceans is neither bleeding-edge technology nor "timing for market entry." Sometimes these exist; more often, however, they do not. Value innovation occurs only when companies align innovation with utility, price, and cost positions. If they fail to anchor innovation with value in this way, technology innovators and market pioneers often lay the eggs that other companies hatch. Value innovation is a new way of thinking about and executing strategy that results in the creation of a blue ocean and a break from the competition. Importantly, value innovation defies one of the most commonly accepted dogmas of competition-based strategy: the value-cost trade-off.20 It is conventionally believed that companies can either create greater value to customers at a higher cost or create reasonable value at a lower cost. Here strategy is seen as making a choice between differentiation and low cost.21 In contrast, those that seek to create blue oceans pursue differentiation and low cost simultaneously. Let's return to the example of Cirque du Soleil. Pursuing differentiation and low cost simultaneously lies at the heart of the entertainment experience it created. At the time of its debut, other circuses focused on benchmarking one another and maximizing their share of already shrinking demand by tweaking traditional circus acts. This included trying to secure more famous clowns and lion tamers, a strategy that raised circuses' cost structure without substantially altering the circus experience. The result was rising costs without rising revenues, and a downward spiral of overall circus demand. These efforts were made irrelevant when Cirque du Soleil appeared. Neither an ordinary circus nor a classic theater production, Cirque du Soleil paid no heed to what the competition did. Instead of following the conventional logic of outpacing the competition by offering a better solution to the given problem—creating a circus with even greater fun and thrills—it sought to offer people the fun and thrill of the circus and the intellectual sophistication and artistic richness of the theater at the same time; hence, it redefined the problem itself.22 By breaking the market boundaries of theater and circus, Cirque du Soleil gained a new understanding not only of circus customers but also of circus noncustomers: adult theater customers. This led to a whole new circus concept that broke the value-cost trade-off and created a blue ocean of new market space. Consider the differences. Whereas other circuses focused on offering animal shows, hiring star performers, presenting multiple show arenas in the form of three rings, and pushing aisle concession sales, Cirque du Soleil did away with all these factors. These factors had long been taken for granted in the traditional circus industry, which never questioned their ongoing relevance. However, there was increasing public discomfort with the use of animals. Moreover, animal acts were one of the most expensive elements, including not only the cost of the animals but also their training, medical care, housing, insurance, and transportation. Similarly, while the circus industry focused on featuring stars, in the mind of the public the so-called stars of the circus were trivial next to movie stars. Again, they were a high-cost component carrying little sway with spectators. Gone, too, are three-ring venues. Not only did this arrangement create angst among spectators as they rapidly switched their gaze from one ring to the other, but it also increased the number of performers needed, with obvious cost implications. And although aisle concession sales appeared to be a good way to generate revenue, in practice the high prices discouraged audiences from making purchases and made them feel they were being taken for a ride. The lasting allure of the traditional circus came down to only three key factors: the tent, the clowns, and the classic acrobatic acts such as the wheelman and short stunts. So Cirque du Soleil kept the clowns but shifted their humor from slapstick to a more enchanting, sophisticated style. It glamorized the tent, an element that, ironically, many circuses had begun to forfeit in favor of rented venues. Seeing that this unique venue symbolically captured the magic of the circus, Cirque du Soleil designed the classic symbol of the circus with a glorious external finish and a higher level of comfort, making its tents reminiscent of the grand epic circuses. Gone were the sawdust and hard benches. Acrobats and other thrilling acts are retained, but their roles were reduced and made more elegant by the addition of artistic flair and intellectual wonder to the acts. By looking across the market boundary of theater, Cirque du Soleil also offered new noncircus factors, such as a story line and, with it, intellectual richness, artistic music and dance, and multiple productions. These factors, entirely new creations for the circus industry, are drawn from the alternative live entertainment industry of theater. Unlike traditional circus shows having a series of unrelated acts, for example, each Cirque du Soleil creation has a theme and story line, somewhat resembling a theater performance. Although the theme is vague (and intentionally so), it brings harmony and an intellectual element to the show—without limiting the potential for acts. Le Cirque also borrows ideas from Broadway shows. For example, it features multiple productions rather than the traditional "one for all" shows. As with Broadway shows, too, each Cirque du Soleil show has an original score and assorted music, which drives the visual performance, lighting, and timing of the acts rather than the other way around. The shows feature abstract and spiritual dance, an idea derived from theater and ballet. By introducing these new factors into its offering, Cirque du Soleil has created more sophisticated shows. Moreover, by injecting the concept of multiple productions and by giving people a reason to come to the circus more frequently, Cirque du Soleil has dramatically increased demand. In short, Cirque du Soleil offers the best of both circus and theater, and it has eliminated or reduced everything else. By offering unprecedented utility, Cirque du Soleil has created a blue ocean and has invented a new form of live entertainment, one that is markedly different from both traditional circus and theater. At the same time, by eliminating many of the most costly elements of the circus, it has dramatically reduced its cost structure, achieving both differentiation and low cost. Le Cirque strategically priced its tickets against those of the theater, lifting the price point of the circus industry by several multiples while still pricing its productions to capture the mass of adult customers, who were used to theater prices .

Value Innovation: The Cornerstone of Blue Ocean Strategy Value innovation is created in the region where a company's actions favorably affect both its cost structure and its value proposition to buyers. Cost savings are made by eliminating and reducing the factors an industry competes on. Buyer value is lifted by raising and creating elements the industry has never offered. Over time, costs are reduced further as scale economies kick in due to the high sales volumes that superior value generates.

the creation of blue oceans is about driving costs down while simultaneously driving value up for buyers. This is how a leap in value for both the company and its buyers is achieved. Because buyer value comes from the utility and price that the company offers to buyers and because the value to the company is generated from price and its cost structure, value innovation is achieved only when the whole system of the company's utility, price, and cost activities is properly aligned. It is this whole-system approach that makes the creation of blue oceans a sustainable strategy. Blue ocean strategy integrates the range of a firm's functional and operational activities. In contrast, innovations such as production innovations can be achieved at the subsystem level without impacting the company's overall strategy. An innovation in the production process, for example, may lower a company's cost structure to reinforce its existing cost leadership strategy without changing the utility proposition of its offering. Although innovations of this sort may help to secure and even lift a company's position in the existing market space, such a subsystem approach will rarely create a blue ocean of new market space. In this sense, value innovation is more than innovation. It is about strategy that embraces the entire system of a company's activities.23 Value innovation requires companies to orient the whole system toward achieving a leap in value for both buyers and themselves. Absent such an integral approach, innovation will remain divided from the core of strategy. outlines the key defining features of red and blue ocean strategies. Competition-based red ocean strategy assumes that an industry's structural conditions are given and that firms are forced to compete within them, an assumption based on what the academics call the structuralist view, or environmental determinism. 25 In contrast, value innovation is based on the view that market boundaries and industry structure are not given and can be reconstructed by the actions and beliefs of industry players.

Red Ocean Versus Blue Ocean Strategy Red Ocean Strategy Blue Ocean Strategy Compete in existing market space. Create uncontested market space. Beat the competition. Make the competition irrelevant. Exploit existing demand. Create and capture new demand. Make the value-cost trade-off. Break the value-cost trade-off. Align the whole system of a firm's activities Align the whole system of a firm's with its strategic choice of differentiation activities in pursuit of differentiation or low cost. and low cost.

We call this the reconstructionist view. In the red ocean, differentiation costs because firms compete with the same best-practice rule. Here, the strategic choices for firms are to pursue either differentiation or low cost. In the reconstructionist world, however, the strategic aim is to create new best-practice rules by breaking the existing valuecost trade-off and thereby creating a blue ocean. (For more discussions on this, see appendix B, "Value Innovation: A Reconstructionist View of Strategy.") Cirque du Soleil broke the best practice rule of the circus industry, achieving both differentiation and low cost by reconstructing elements across existing industry boundaries. Is Cirque du Soleil, then, really a circus, with all that it eliminated, reduced, raised, and created? Or is it theater? And if it is theater, then what genre— a Broadway show, an opera, a ballet? It is not clear. Cirque du Soleil reconstructed elements across these alternatives, and, in the end, it is simultaneously a little of all of them and none of any of them in their entirety. It created a blue ocean of new, uncontested market space that as of yet has no agreed-on industry name.

CHAPTER THREE

DISCOVERING POWER

The second natural advantage of many good strategies comes from insight into new sources of strength and weakness. Looking at things from a different or fresh perspective can reveal new realms of advantage and opportunity as well as weakness and threat. A SLUNG STONE In about 1030 B.C., David the shepherd boy defeated the warrior Goliath. When Goliath stepped from the ranks of the Philistines and shouted a challenge, the army of King Saul cringed in terror. Goliath was over nine feet tall, his spear like a weaver's beam. His bronze helmet and body armor shone in the sunlight. David was not old enough to soldier like his brothers, yet nonetheless wanted to face the giant. Saul advised David that he was too young and the giant a skilled veteran, but relented and gave him armor. The armor was heavy and David discarded it, rushing to combat in shepherd's garb. Moving toward Goliath, he took a stone and launched it with his sling. Struck in the forehead, Goliath fell dead on the spot. David moved forward and took the fallen champion's head. The Philistines fled. It is said that strategy brings relative strength to bear against relative weakness. Let's follow the advice of countless articles and textbooks and make a list of David's and Goliath's apparent strengths and weaknesses: This mismatch must have been Saul's concern as he tried to hold David back, then relented and gave him armor. In the story, it is only after the stone is slung that the listener's viewpoint shifts and one realizes that the boy's experience with a shepherd's sling is a strength, as is his youthful quickness. Then the listener realizes that David discarded the armor because it would only slow him down; had he come close enough to receive a blow from the giant, bronze armor would not have saved him. Finally, when the stone strikes Goliath's forehead, the listener suddenly discovers a critical weakness—Goliath's armor didn't cover this vital area. David's weapon delivered force with precision over a distance, neutering Goliath's supposed advantages of size and strength. The story teaches us that our preconceived ideas of strength and weakness may be unsound. It is the victory of apparent weakness over apparent strength that gives this tale its bite. More than the deft wielding of power, the listener experiences the actual discovery of power in a situation—the creation or revelation of a decisive asymmetry. How someone can see what others have not, or what they have ignored, and thereby discover a pivotal objective and create an advantage, lies at the very edge of our understanding, something glimpsed only out of the corner of our minds. Not every good strategy draws on this kind of insight, but those that do generate the extra kick that separates "ordinary excellence" from the extraordinary. WAL-MART Much of my work with MBA students and companies involves helping them uncover the hidden power in situations. As part of this process I often teach a case about Wal-Mart's founding and rise, ending in 1986 with Sam Walton as the richest person in the United States. 1 In a subsequent session I will follow up by discussing the modern Wal-Mart, pushing into urban areas, stretching out to Europe, and becoming the largest corporation on the planet in terms of revenue. But the older case portrays a simpler, leaner Wal-Mart—a youthful challenger rather than the behemoth it has become. Hard as it is to believe today, Wal-Mart was once David, not Goliath. Before beginning the discussion, I copy a phrase from the case onto the whiteboard and draw a box around it: CONVENTIONAL WISDOM: A full-line discount store needs a population base of at least 100,000. The question for the group is simple: Why has Wal-Mart been so successful? To start, I call on Bill, who had some experience in sales during the earlier part of his career. He begins with the ritual invocation of founder Sam Walton's leadership. Neither agreeing nor disagreeing, I write "Sam Walton" on the board and press him further. "What did Walton do that made a difference?" Bill looks at my labeled box on the board and says, "Walton broke the conventional wisdom. He put big stores in small towns. Wal-Mart had everyday low prices. Wal-Mart ran a computerized warehousing and trucking system to manage the movement of stock into stores. It was nonunion. It had low administrative expenses." It takes about thirty minutes for six other participants to flesh out this list. They are willing to throw anything into the bin, and I don't stop them. I prod for detail and context, asking, "How big were the stores?" "How small were the towns?" "How did the computerized logistics system work?" And "What did Wal-Mart do to keep its administrative expenses so low?" As the responses flood in, three diagrams take shape on the whiteboard. A circle appears, representing a small town of ten thousand persons. A large box drawn in the circle represents a fortyfive-thousand-square-foot Wal-Mart store. A second diagram of the logistical system emerges. A square box represents a regional distribution center. From the box, a line marks the path of a truck, swooping out to pass by some of the 150 stores served by the distribution center. On the return path, the line passes vendors, picking up pallets of goods. The line plunges back to the square, where an "X" denotes cross-docking to an outgoing truck. Lines of a different color depict the data flows, from the store to a central computer, and then out to vendors and the distribution center. Finally, as we discuss the management system, I draw the paths of the regional managers as they follow a weekly circuit: Fly out from Bentonville, Arkansas, on Monday, visit stores, pick up and distribute information, and return to Bentonville on Thursday for group meetings on Friday and Saturday. The last two diagrams are eerily similar—both revealing the hub structure of efficient distribution. The discussion slows. We have gotten most of the facts out. I look around the room, trying to include them all, and say, "If the policies you have listed are the reasons for Wal-Mart's success, and if this case was published—let's see—in 1986, then why was the company able to run rampant over Kmart for the next decade? Wasn't the formula obvious? Where was the competition?" Silence. This question breaks the pleasant give-and-take of reciting case facts. The case actually says almost nothing about competition, referring broadly to the discounting industry. But surely executives and MBA students would have thought about this in preparing for this discussion. Yet it is totally predictable that they will not. Because the case does not focus on competition, neither do they. I know it will turn out this way—it always does. Half of what alert participants learn in a strategy exercise is to consider the competition even when no one tells you to do it in advance. Looking just at the actions of a winning firm, you see only part of the picture. Whenever an organization succeeds greatly, there is also, at the same time, either blocked or failed competition. Sometimes competition is blocked because an innovator holds a patent or some other legal claim to a temporary monopoly. But there may also be a natural reason imitation is difficult or very costly. WalMart's advantage must stem from something that competitors cannot easily copy, or do not copy because of inertia and incompetence. In the case of Wal-Mart, the principal competitive failure was Kmart. Originally named the S. S. Kresge Corporation, Kmart was once the leader in low-cost variety retailing. It spent much of the 1970s and 1980s expanding internationally and ignoring

WalMart's innovations in logistics and its growing dominance of small-town discounting. It filed for bankruptcy in 2002. After some moments I ask a more pointed question: "Both Wal-Mart and Kmart began to install bar-code scanners at cash registers in the early 1980s. Why did Wal-Mart seem to benefit from this more than Kmart?" First used in grocery supermarkets, bar-code scanners at retail checkout stations are now ubiquitous. Mass merchandisers began to use them in the early 1980s. Most retailers saw the barcode scanner as a way of eliminating the cost of constantly changing the price stickers on items. But Wal-Mart went further, developing its own satellite-based information systems. Then it used this data to manage its inbound logistics system and traded it with suppliers in return for discounts. Susan, a human resources executive, suddenly perks up. Isolating one small policy has triggered a thought. I gave a talk the day before on "complementary" policies and she sees the connection. "By itself," she says, "it doesn't help that much. Kmart would have to move the data to distribution centers and suppliers. It would have to operate an integrated inbound logistics system." "Good," I say, and point out to everyone that Wal-Mart's policies fit together—the bar codes, the integrated logistics, the frequent just-in-time deliveries, the large stores with low inventory—they are complements to one another, forming an integrated design. This whole design—structure, policies, and actions—is coherent. Each part of the design is shaped and specialized to the others. The pieces are not interchangeable parts. Many competitors do not have much of a design, shaping each of their elements around some imagined "best practice" form. Others will have more coherence but will have aimed their designs at different purposes. In either case, such competitors will have difficulty in dealing with Wal-Mart. Copying elements of its strategy piecemeal, there will be little benefit. A competitor would have to adopt the whole design, not just a part of it. There is much more to be discussed: first-mover advantages, quantifying its cost advantage, the issue of competence and learning developed over time, the function of leadership, and whether this design can work in cities. We proceed. With fifteen minutes to go, I let the discussion wind down. They have done a good job analyzing Wal-Mart's business, and I say so. But, I tell them, there is one more thing. Something I barely understand but that seems important. It has to do with the "conventional wisdom"—the phrase from the case I put on the whiteboard at the beginning of the class: "A full-line discount store needs a population base of at least 100,000." I turn to Bill and say: "You started us out by arguing that Walton broke the conventional wisdom. But the conventional wisdom was based on the straightforward logic of fixed and variable cost. It takes a lot of customers to spread the overhead and keep costs and prices low. Exactly how did Walton break the iron logic of cost?" I push ahead, putting Bill into a role: "I want you to imagine that you are a Wal-Mart store manager. It's 1985 and you are unhappy with the whole company. You feel that they don't understand your town. You complain to your dad, and he says, 'Why don't we just buy them out? We can run the store ourselves.' Assuming Dad has the resources, what do you think of his proposal?" Bill blinks, surprised at being put on the spot for a second time. He thinks a bit, then says, "No, it's not a good idea. We couldn't make a go of it alone. The Wal-Mart store needs to be part of the network." I turn back the whiteboard and stand right next to the boxed principle: "A full-line discount store needs a population base of at least 100,000." I repeat his phrase, "The Wal-Mart store needs to be part of the network," while drawing a circle around the word "store." Then I wait. With luck, someone will get it. As one student tries to articulate the discovery, others get it, and I sense a small avalanche of "ahas," like a pot of corn kernels suddenly popping. It isn't the store; it is the network of 150 stores. And the data flows and the management flows and a distribution hub. The network replaced the store. A regional network of 150 stores serves a population of millions! Walton didn't break the conventional wisdom; he broke the old definition of a store. If no one gets it right away, I drop hints until they do. When you understand that Walton redefined the notion of "store," your view of how Wal-Mart's policies fit together undergoes a subtle shift. You begin to see the interdependencies among location decisions. Store locations express the economics of the network, not just the pull of demand. You also see the balance of power at Wal-Mart. The individual store has little negotiating power—its options are limited. Most crucially, the network, not the store, became Wal-Mart's basic unit of management. In making an integrated network into the operating unit of the company, instead of the individual store, Walton broke with an even deeper conventional wisdom of his era: the doctrine of decentralization, that each kettle should sit on its own bottom. Kmart had long adhered to this doctrine, giving each store manager authority to choose product lines, pick vendors, and set prices. After all, we are told that decentralization is a good thing. But the oft-forgotten cost of decentralization is lost coordination across units. Stores that do not choose the same vendors or negotiate the same terms cannot benefit from an integrated network of data and transport. Stores that do not share detailed information about what works and what does not cannot benefit from one another's learning. If your competitors also operate this kind of decentralized system, little may be lost. But once Walton's insights made the decentralized structure a disadvantage, Kmart had a severe problem. A large organization may balk at adopting a new technique, but such change is manageable. But breaking with doctrine—with one's basic philosophy—is rare absent a near-death experience. The hidden power of Wal-Mart's strategy came from a shift in perspective. Lacking that perspective, Kmart saw Wal-Mart like Goliath saw David—smaller and less experienced in the big leagues. But Wal-Mart's advantages were not inherent in its history or size. They grew out of a subtle shift in how to think about discount retailing. Tradition saw discounting as tied to urban densities, whereas Sam Walton saw a way to build efficiency by embedding each store in a network of computing and logistics. Today we call this supply-chain management, but in 1984 it was as an unexpected shift in viewpoint. And it had the impact of David's slung stone.

Analytical Tools and Frameworks

Developing a set of analytical tools and frameworks in an attempt to make the formulation and execution of blue ocean strategy as systematic and actionable as competing in the red waters of known market space. These analytics fill a central void in the field of strategy, which has developed an impressive array of tools and frameworks to compete in red oceans, such as the five forces for analyzing existing industry conditions and three generic strategies, but has remained virtually silent on practical tools to excel in blue oceans. Instead, executives have received calls to be brave and entrepreneurial, to learn from failure, and to seek out revolutionaries. Although thought-provoking, these are not substitutes for analytics to navigate successfully in blue waters. In the absence of analytics, executives cannot be expected to act on the call to break out of existing competition. Effective blue ocean strategy should be about risk minimization and not risk taking.To address this imbalance, we studied companies around the world and developed practical methodologies in the quest of blue oceans. We then applied and tested these tools and frameworks in action by working with companies in their pursuit of blue oceans, enriching and refining them in the process. The tools and frameworks presented here are used throughout this book as we discuss the six principles of formulating and executing blue ocean strategy. As a brief introduction to these tools and frameworks, let's look at one industry—the U.S. wine industry—to see how these tools can be applied in practice in the creation of blue oceans. The United States has the third largest aggregate consumption of wine worldwide. Yet the $20 billion industry is intensely competitive. California wines dominate the domestic market, capturing two-thirds of all U.S. wine sales. These wines compete head-to-head with imported wines from France, Italy, and Spain and New

World wines from countries such as Chile, Australia, and Argentina, which have increasingly targeted the U.S. market. With the supply of wines increasing from Oregon, Washington, and New York state and with newly mature vineyard plantings in California, the number of wines has exploded. Yet the U.S. consumer base has essentially remained stagnant. The United States remains stuck at thirty-first place in world per capita wine consumption. The intense competition has fueled ongoing industry consolidation. The top eight companies produce more than 75 percent of the wine in the United States, and the estimated one thousand six hundred other wineries produce the remaining 25 percent. The dominance of a few key players allows them to leverage distributors to gain shelf space and put millions of dollars into above-the-line marketing budgets. There is a simultaneous consolidation of retailers and distributors across the United States, something that raises their bargaining power against the plethora of wine makers. Titanic battles are being fought for retail and distribution space. It is no surprise that weak, poorly run companies are increasingly being swept aside. Downward pressure on wine prices has set in.In short, the U.S. wine industry faces intense competition, mounting price pressure, increasing bargaining power on the part of retail and distribution channels, and flat demand despite overwhelming choice. Following conventional strategic thinking, the industry is hardly attractive. For strategists, the critical question is, How do you break out of this red ocean of bloody competition to make the competition irrelevant? How do you open up and capture a blue ocean of uncontested market space? To address these questions, we turn to the strategy canvas, an analytic framework that is central to value innovation and the creation of blue oceans. The Strategy Canvas The strategy canvas is both a diagnostic and an action framework for building a compelling blue ocean strategy. It serves two purposes. First, it captures the current state of play in the known market space. This allows you to understand where the competition is currently investing, the factors the industry currently competes on in products, service, and delivery, and what customers receive from the existing competitive offerings on the market. Figure 2-1 captures all this information in graphic form. The horizontal axis captures the range of factors the industry competes on and invests in. In the case of the U.S. wine industry, there are seven principal factors: • Price per bottle of wine • An elite, refined image in packaging, including labels announcing the wine medals won and the use of esoteric enological terminology to stress the art and science of wine making •

Above-the-line marketing to raise consumer awareness in a crowded market and to encourage distributors and retailers to give prominence to a particular wine houseAging quality of wine • The prestige of a wine's vineyard and its legacy (hence the appellations of estates and chateaux and references to the historic age of the establishment) • The complexity and sophistication of a wine's taste, including such things as tannins and oak • A diverse range of wines to cover all varieties of grapes and consumer preferences from Chardonnay to Merlot, and so on These factors are viewed as key to the promotion of wine as a unique beverage for the informed wine drinker, worthy of special occasions. That is the underlying structure of the U.S. wine industry from the market perspective. Now let's turn to the vertical axis of the strategy canvas, which captures the offering level that buyers receive across all these key competing factors. A high score means that a company offers buyers more, and hence invests more, in that factor. In the case of price, a higher score indicates a higher price. We can now plot the current offering of wineries across all these factors to understand wineries' strategic profiles, or value curves. The value curve, the basic component of the strategy canvas, is a graphic depiction of a company's relative performance across its industry's factors of competition. Figure 2 1 shows that, although more than one thousand six hundred wineries participate in the U.S. wine industry, from the buyer's point of view there is enormous convergence in their value curves. Despite the plethora of competitors, when premium brand wines are plotted on the strategy canvas we discover that from the market point of view all of them essentially have the same strategic profile. They offer a high price and present a high level of offering across all the key competing factors. Their strategic profile follows a classic differentiation strategy. From the market point of view, however, they are all different in the same way. On the other hand, budget wines also have the same essential strategic profile. Their price is low, as is their offering across all the key competing factors. These are classic low-cost players. Moreover, the value curves of premium and low-cost wines share the same basic shape. The two strategic groups' strategies march in lockstep, but at different altitudes of offering level. To set a company on a strong, profitable growth trajectory in the face of these industry conditions, it won't work to benchmark competitors and try to outcompete them by offering a little more for a little less. Such a strategy may nudge sales up but will hardly drive a company to open up uncontested market space. Nor is conducting extensive customer research the path to blue oceans. Our research found that customers can scarcely imagine how to create uncontested market space. Their insight also tends toward the familiar "offer me more for less." And what customers typically want "more" of are those product and service features that the industry currently offers. strategy canvas, which captures the offering level that buyers receive across all these key competing factors. A high score means that a company offers buyers more, and hence invests more, in that factor. In the case of price, a higher score indicates a higher price. We can now plot the current offering of wineries across all these factors to understand wineries' strategic profiles, or value curves. To fundamentally shift the strategy canvas of an industry, you must begin by reorienting your strategic focus from competitors to alternatives, and from customers to noncustomers of the industry.1 To pursue both value and cost, you should resist the old logic of benchmarking competitors in the existing field and choosing between differentiation and cost leadership. As you shift your strategic focus from current competition to alternatives and noncustomers, you gain insight into how to redefine the problem the industry focuses on and thereby reconstruct buyer value elements that reside across industry boundaries. Conventional strategic logic, by contrast, drives you to offer better solutions than your rivals to existing problems defined by your industry. In the case of the U.S. wine industry, conventional wisdom caused wineries to focus on overdelivering on prestige and the quality of wine at its price point. Overdelivery meant adding complexity to the wine based on taste profiles shared by wine makers and reinforced by the wine show judging system. Wine makers, show judges, and knowledgeable drinkers concur that complexity—layered personality and characteristics that reflect the uniqueness of the soil, season, and wine maker's skill in tannins, oak, and aging processes—equates with quality. By looking across alternatives, however, Casella Wines, an Australian winery, redefined the problem of the wine industry to a new one: how to make a fun and nontraditional wine that's easy to drink for everyone. Why? In looking at the demand side of the alternatives of beer, spirits, and ready-to-drink cocktails, which captured three times as many U.S. consumer alcohol sales as wine, Casella Wines found that the mass of American adults saw wine as a turnoff. It was intimidating and pretentious, and the complexity of wine's taste created flavor challenges for the average person even though it was the basis on which the industry fought to excel. With this insight, Casella Wines was ready to explore how to redraw the strategic profile of the U.S. wine industry to create a blue ocean. To achieve this, it turned to the second basic analytic underlying blue oceans: the four actions framework.

To reconstruct buyer value elements in crafting a new value curve, we have developed the four actions framework. As shown in figure 2-2, to break the trade-off between differentiation and low cost and to create a new value curve, there are four key questions to challenge an industry's strategic logic and business model: • Which of the factors that the industry takes for granted should be eliminated? • Which factors should be reduced well below the industry's standard? • Which factors should be raised well above the industry's standard? • Which factors should be created that the industry has never offered?

The first question forces you to consider eliminating factors that companies in your industry have long competed on. Often those factors are taken for granted even though they no longer have value or may even detract from value. Sometimes there is a fundamental change in what buyers value, but companies that are focused on benchmarking one another do not act on, or even perceive, the change. The second question forces you to determine whether products or services have been overdesigned in the race to match and beat the competition. Here, companies overserve customers, increasing their cost structure for no gain. The third question pushes you to uncover and eliminate the compromises your industry forces customers to make. The fourth question helps you to discover entirely new sources of value for buyers and to create new demand and shift the strategic pricing of the industry. It is by pursuing the first two questions (of eliminating and reducing) that you gain insight into how to drop your cost structure vis-à-vis competitors. Our research has found that rarely do managers systematically set out to eliminate and reduce their investments in factors that an industry competes on. The result is mounting cost structures and complex business models. The second two factors, by contrast, provide you with insight into how to lift buyer value and create new demand. Collectively, they allow you to systematically explore how you can reconstruct buyer value elements across alternative industries to offer buyers an entirely new experience, while simultaneously keeping your cost structure low. Of particular importance are the actions of eliminating and creating, which push companies to go beyond value maximization exercises with existing factors of competition. Eliminating and creating prompt companies to change the factors themselves, hence making the existing rules of competition irrelevant. When you apply the four actions framework to the strategy canvas of your industry, you get a revealing new look at old perceived truths. In the case of the U.S. wine industry, by thinking in terms of these four actions vis-à-vis the current industry logic and looking across alternatives and noncustomers, Casella Wines created [yellow tail], a wine whose strategic profile broke from the competition and created a blue ocean. Instead of offering wine as wine, Casella created a social drink accessible to everyone: beer drinkers, cocktail drinkers, and other drinkers of nonwine beverages. In the space of two years, the fun, social drink [yellow tail] emerged as the fastest growing brand in the histories of both the Australian and the U.S. wine industries and the number one imported wine into the United States, surpassing the wines of France and Italy. By August 2003 it was the number one red wine in a 750-ml bottle sold in the United States, outstripping California labels. By mid-2003, [yellow tail]'s moving average annual sales were tracking at 4.5 million cases. In the context of a global wine glut, [yellow tail] has been racing to keep up with sales. What's more, whereas large wine companies developed strong brands over decades of marketing investment, [yellow tail] leapfrogged tall competitors with no promotional campaign, mass media, or consumer advertising. It didn't simply steal sales from competitors; it grew the market. [yellow tail] brought nonwine drinkers— beer and ready-to-drink cocktail consumers—into the wine market. Moreover, novice table wine drinkers started to drink wine more frequently, jug wine drinkers moved up, and drinkers of more expensive wines moved down to become consumers of [yellow tail].

the extent to which the application of these four actions led to a break from the competition in the U.S. wine industry. Here we can graphically compare [yellow tail]'s blue ocean strategy with the more than one thousand six hundred wineries competing in the United States.]

[yellow tail]'s value curve stands apart. Casella Wines acted on all four actions—eliminate, reduce, raise, and create—to unlock uncontested market space that changed the face of the U.S. wine industry in a span of two years. By looking at the alternatives of beer and ready-to-drink cocktails and thinking in terms of noncustomers, Casella Wines created three new factors in the U.S. wine industry—easy drinking, easy to select, and fun and adventure—and eliminated or reduced everything else. Casella Wines found that the mass of Americans rejected wine because its complicated taste was difficult to appreciate. Beer and ready-to-drink cocktails, for example, were much sweeter and easier to drink. Accordingly, [yellow tail] was a completely new combination of wine characteristics that produced an uncomplicated wine structure that was instantly appealing to the mass of alcohol drinkers. The wine was soft in taste and approachable like ready-to-drink cocktails and beer, and had up-front, primary flavors and pronounced fruit flavors. The sweet fruitiness of the wine also kept people's palate fresher, allowing them to enjoy another glass of wine without thinking about it. The result was an easydrinking wine that did not require years to develop an appreciation for.

In line with this simple fruity sweetness, [yellow tail] dramatically reduced or eliminated all the factors the wine industry had long competed on—tannins, oak, complexity, and aging—in crafting fine wine, whether it was for the premium or the budget segment. With the need for aging eliminated, the needed working capital for aging wine at Casella Wines was also reduced, creating a faster payback for the wine produced. The wine industry criticized the sweet fruitiness of [yellow tail] wine, seeing it as significantly lowering the quality of wine and working against proper appreciation of fine grapes and historic wine craftsmanship. These claims may have been true, but customers of all sorts loved the wine. Wine retailers in the United States offered buyers aisles of wine varieties, but to the general consumer the choice was overwhelming and intimidating. The bottles looked the same, labels were complicated with enological terminology understandable only to the wine connoisseur or hobbyist, and the choice was so extensive that salesclerks at retail shops were at an equal disadvantage in understanding or recommending wine to bewildered potential buyers. Moreover, the rows of wine choice fatigued and demotivated customers, making selection a difficult process that left the average wine purchaser insecure with the choice. [yellow tail] changed all that by creating ease of selection. It dramatically reduced the range of wines offered, creating only two: Chardonnay, the most popular white in the United States, and a red, Shiraz. It removed all technical jargon from the bottles and created instead a striking, simple, and nontraditional label featuring a kangaroo in bright, vibrant colors of orange and yellow on a black background. The wine boxes [yellow tail] came in were also of the same vibrant colors, with the name [yellow tail] printed boldly on the sides; the boxes served the dual purpose of acting as eyecatching, unintimidating displays for the wine. [yellow tail] hit a home run in ease of selection when it made retail shop employees the ambassadors of [yellow tail] by giving them Australian outback clothing, including bushman's hats and oilskin jackets to wear at work. The retail employees were inspired by the branded clothing and having a wine they themselves did not feel intimidated by, and recommendations to buy [yellow tail] flew out of their mouths. In short, it was fun to recommend [yellow tail]. The simplicity of offering only two wines at the start—a red and a white—streamlined Casella Wines' business model. Minimizing the stockkeeping units maximized its stock turnover and minimized investment in warehouse inventory. In fact, this reduction of variety was carried over to the bottles inside the cases. [yellow tail] broke industry conventions. Casella Wines was the first company to put both red and white wine in the same-shaped bottle, a practice that created further simplicity in manufacturing and purchasing and resulted in stunningly simple wine displays. The wine industry worldwide was proud to promote wine as a refined beverage with a long history and tradition. This is reflected in the target market for the United States: educated professionals in the upper income brackets. Hence, the continuous focus on the quality and legacy of the vineyard, the chateau's or estate's historical tradition, and the wine medals won. Indeed the growth strategies of the major players in the U.S. wine industry were targeted at the premium end of the market, with tens of millions invested in brand advertising to strengthen this image. By looking to beer and ready-to-drink cocktail customers, however, [yellow tail] found that this elite image did not resonate with the general public, which found it intimidating. So [yellow tail] broke with tradition and created a personality that embodied the characteristics of the Australian culture: bold, laid back, fun, and adventurous. Approachability was the mantra: "The essence of a great land . . . Australia." There was no traditional winery image. The lowercase spelling of the name [yellow tail], coupled with the vibrant colors and the kangaroo motif, echoed Australia. And indeed no reference to the vineyard was made on the bottle. The wine promised to jump from the glass like an Aussie kangaroo. The result is that [yellow tail] appealed to a broad cross section of alcohol beverage consumers. By offering this leap in value, [yel low tail] raised the price of its wines above the budget market, pricing them at $6.99 a bottle, more than double the price of a jug wine. From the moment the wine hit the retail shelves in July 2001, sales took off. The Eliminate-Reduce-Raise-Create Grid There is a third tool that is key to creation of blue oceans. It is a supplementary analytic to the four actions framework called the eliminate-reduce-raise-create grid . The grid pushes companies not only to ask all four questions in the four actions framework but also to act on all four to create a new value curve. By driving companies to fill in the grid with the actions of eliminating and reducing as well as raising and creating, the grid gives companies four immediate benefits: • It pushes them to simultaneously pursue differentiation and low costs to break the value-cost trade-off.

It immediately flags companies that are focused only on raising and creating and thereby lifting their cost structure and often overengineering products and services—a common plight in many companies. • It is easily understood by managers at any level, creating a high level of engagement in its application. • Because completing the grid is a challenging task, it drives companies to robustly scrutinize every factor the industry competes on, making them discover the range of implicit assumptions they make unconsciously in competing

Three Characteristics of a Good Strategy [yellow tail], like Cirque du Soleil, created a unique and exceptional value curve to unlock a blue ocean. As shown in the strategy canvas, [yellow tail]'s value curve has focus; the company does not diffuse its efforts across all key factors of competition. The shape of its value curve diverges from the other players', a result of not benchmarking competitors but instead looking across alternatives. The tagline of [yellow tail]'s strategic profile is clear: a fun and simple wine to be enjoyed every day. When expressed through a value curve, then, an effective blue ocean strategy like [yellow tail]'s has three complementary qualities: focus, divergence, and a compelling tagline. Without these qualities, a company's strategy will likely be muddled, undifferentiated, and hard to communicate with a high cost structure. The four actions of creating a new value curve should be well guided toward building a company's strategic profile with these characteristics. These three characteristics serve as an initial litmus test of the commercial viability of blue ocean ideas. A look at Southwest Airlines' strategic profile illustrates how these three qualities underlie the company's effective strategy in reinventing the short-haul airline industry via value innovation Southwest Airlines created a blue ocean by breaking the trade-offs customers had to make between the speed of airplanes and the economy and flexibility of car transport. To achieve this, Southwest offered high-speed transport with frequent and flexible departures at prices attractive to the mass of buyers. By eliminating and reducing certain factors of competition and raising others in the traditional airline industry, as well as by creating new factors drawn from the alternative industry of car transport, Southwest Airlines was able to offer unprecedented utility for air travelers and achieve a leap in value with a low-cost business model. The value curve of Southwest Airlines differs distinctively from those of its competitors in the strategy canvas. Its strategic profile is a typical example of a compelling blue ocean strategy.

Focus Every great strategy has focus, and a company's strategic profile, or value curve, should clearly show it. Looking at Southwest's profile, we can see at once that the company emphasizes only three factors: friendly service, speed, and frequent point-to-point departures. By focusing in this way, Southwest has been able to price against car transportation; it doesn't make extra investments in meals, lounges, and seating choices. By contrast, Southwest's traditional competitors invest in all the airline industry's competitive factors, making it much more difficult for them to match Southwest's prices. Investing across the board, these companies let their competitors' moves set their own agendas. Costly business models result. Divergence When a company's strategy is formed reactively as it tries to keep up with the competition, it loses its uniqueness. Consider the similarities in most airlines' meals and business-class lounges. On the strategy canvas, therefore, reactive strategists tend to share the same strategic profile. Indeed, in the case of Southwest, the value curves of the company's competitors are virtually identical and therefore can be summarized on the strategy canvas with a single value curve. In contrast, the value curves of blue ocean strategists always stand apart. By applying the four actions of eliminating, reducing, raising, and creating, they differentiate their profiles from the industry's average profile. Southwest, for example, pioneered pointto-point travel between midsize cities; previously, the industry operated through hub-and-spoke systems. Compelling Tagline A good strategy has a clear-cut and compelling tagline. "The speed of a plane at the price of a car—whenever you need it." That's the tagline of Southwest Airlines, or at least it could be. What couldSouthwest's competitors say? Even the most proficient ad agency would have difficulty reducing the conventional offering of lunches, seat choices, lounges, and hub links, with standard service, slower speeds, and higher prices into a memorable tagline. A good tagline must not only deliver a clear message but also advertise an offering truthfully, or else customers will lose trust and interest. In fact, a good way to test the effectiveness and strength of a strategy is to look at whether it contains a strong and authentic tagline. Cirque du Soleil's strategic profile also meets the three criteria that define blue ocean strategy: focus, divergence, and a compelling tagline. Cirque du Soleil's strategy canvas allows us to graphically compare its strategic profile with those of its major competitors. The canvas shows clearly the extent of Cirque du Soleil's departure from the conventional logic of the circus. The figure shows that the value curve of Ringling Bros. and Barnum & Bailey is the same basic shape as those of smaller regional circuses. The main difference is that regional circuses offer less of each competing factor because of their restricted resources. By contrast, Cirque du Soleil's value curve stands apart. It has new and noncircus factors such as theme, multiple productions, refined watching environment, and artistic music and dance. These factors, entirely new creations for the circus industry, are drawn from the alternative live entertainment industry of theater. In this way, the strategy canvas clearly depicts the traditional factors that affect competition among industry players, as well as new factors that lead to creation of new market space and that shift the strategy canvas of an industry. [yellow tail], Cirque du Soleil, and Southwest Airlines created blue oceans in very different business situations and industrial contexts. However, their strategic profiles shared the same three characteristics: focus, divergence, and a compelling tagline. These three criteria guide companies in carrying out the process of reconstruction to arrive at a breakthrough in value both for buyers and for themselves. Reading the Value Curves The strategy canvas enables companies to see the future in the present. To achieve this, companies must understand how to read value curves. Embedded in the value curves of an industry is a wealth of strategic knowledge on the current status and future of a business. A Blue Ocean Strategy The first question the value curves answer is whether a business deserves to be a winner. When a company's value curve, or its competitors', meets the three criteria that define a good blue ocean strategy—focus, divergence, and a compelling tagline that speaks to the market—the company is on the right track. These three criteria serve as an initial litmus test of the commercial viability of blue ocean ideas.

On the other hand, when a company's value curve lacks focus, its cost structure will tend to be high and its business model complex in implementation and execution. When it lacks divergence, a company's strategy is a me-too, with no reason to stand apart in the marketplace. When it lacks a compelling tagline that speaks to buyers, it is likely to be internally driven or a classic example of innovation for innovation's sake with no great commercial potential and no natural take-off capability. A Company Caught in the Red Ocean When a company's value curve converges with its competitors, it signals that a company is likely caught within the red ocean of bloody competition. A company's explicit or implicit strategy tends to be trying to outdo its competition on the basis of cost or quality. This signals slow growth unless, by the grace of luck, the company benefits from being in an industry that is growing on its own accord. This growth is not due to a company's strategy, however, but to luck. Overdelivery Without Payback When a company's value curve on the strategy canvas is shown to deliver high levels across all factors, the question is, Does the company's market share and profitability reflect these investments? If not, the strategy canvas signals that the company may be oversupplying its customers, offering too much of those elements that add incremental value to buyers. To value-innovate, the company must decide which factors to eliminate and reduce—and not only those to raise and create—to construct a divergent value curve. An Incoherent Strategy When a company's value curve looks like a bowl of spaghetti—a zigzag with no rhyme or reason, where the offering can be described as "low-high-low-low-high-low-high"—it signals that the company doesn't have a coherent strategy. Its strategy is likely based on independent substrategies. These may individually make sense and keep the business running and everyone busy, but collectively they do little to distinguish the company from the best competitor or to provide a clear strategic vision. This is often a reflection of an organization with divisional or functional silos. Strategic Contradictions Are there strategic contradictions? These are areas where a company is offering a high level on one competing factor while ignoring others that support that factor. An example is investing heavily in making a company's Web site easy to use but failing to correct the site's slow speed of operation. Strategic inconsistencies can also be found between the level of your offering and your price. For example, a petroleum station company found that it offered "less for more": fewer services than the best competitor at a higher price. No wonder it was losing market share fast. An Internally Driven Company In drawing the strategy canvas, how does a company label the industry's competing factors? For example, does it use the word megahertz instead of speed, or thermal water temperature instead of hot water? Are the competing factors stated in terms buyers can understand and value, or are they in operational jargon? The kind of language used in the strategy canvas gives insight as to whether a company's strategic vision is built on an "outside-in" perspective, driven by the demand side, or an "inside-out" perspective that is operationally driven. Analyzing the language of the strategy canvas helps a company understand how far it is from creating industry demand. The tools and frameworks introduced here are essential analytics used throughout this book, and supplementary tools are introduced in other chapters as needed. It is the intersection between these analytic techniques and the six principles of formulating and executing blue oceans that allow companies to break from the competition and unlock uncontested market space. Now we move on to the first principle, reconstructing market boundaries. In the next chapter we discuss the opportunity-maximizing and risk-minimizing paths to creating blue oceans.

CHAPTER FIVE

BAD STRATEGY

Bad strategy is not simply the absence of good strategy. It grows out of specific misconceptions and leadership dysfunctions. Once you develop the ability to detect bad strategy, you will dramatically improve your effectiveness at judging, influencing, and creating strategy. To detect a bad strategy, look for one or more of its four major hallmarks: • Fluf . Fluff is a form of gibberish masquerading as strategic concepts or arguments. It uses "Sunday" words (words that are inflated and unnecessarily abstruse) and apparently esoteric concepts to create the illusion of high-level thinking. • Failure to face the challenge. Bad strategy fails to recognize or define the challenge. When you cannot define the challenge, you cannot evaluate a strategy or improve it. • Mistaking goals for strategy. Many bad strategies are just statements of desire rather than plans for overcoming obstacles. • Bad strategic objectives. A strategic objective is set by a leader as a means to an end. Strategic objectives are "bad" when they fail to address critical issues or when they are impracticable.

There was no disagreement about the facts. During and after World War II, especially with the advent of nuclear weapons, U.S. national leadership took national security strategy very seriously. But after 1989, as the threat of a major offensive attack by another large power faded, the need for a new integrated strategic review of U.S. national security strategy became apparent. A new post–Cold War strategy was needed, one that would deal with issues such as nuclear proliferation, infrastructure protection, the use of space, energy use and supply, global financial markets, the information revolution, advances in biotechnology, the future of NATO, ethnic conflicts and failing states, and difficulties with Russia and China. This need for a dramatic redesign of the United States'security-oriented institutional structures and processes became even more important following the September 11, 2001, attacks. One analysis, the Princeton Project on

National Security, succinctly described the situation: "While the Bush administration's 2002 National Security Strategy did articulate a set of U.S. national goals and objectives, it was not the product of a serious attempt at strategic planning.... The articulation of a national vision that describes America's purpose in the post–September 11th world is useful— indeed, it is vital—but describing a destination is no substitute for developing a comprehensive roadmap for how the country will achieve its stated goals." 2 Despite the obvious need, very little had been done. The central question on the table was "Why not?" Was it a problem of leadership, institutional structure, or shortened time horizons? The seminar was guided by a fascinating paper arguing that there had been a general decline in competence at understanding and formulating strategy. 3 It contended, "All too much of what is put forward as strategy is not. The basic problem is confusion between strategy and strategic goals." With regard to the recent editions of the national security strategy, it said "when you look closely at either the 2002 or 2006 documents, all you find are lists of goals and sub-goals, not strategies." Reading the documents referenced, I had to agree. 4 They presented a plethora of broad goals and affirmations of values such as democracy and economic well-being. But there was little guidance as to how to actually deal with the national security situation. At the center of these documents lay President George W. Bush's dramatic new doctrine of responding to the threat of weapons of mass destruction with preventive war, if necessary. Yet there were no indications that this doctrine had been turned into a coherent strategy. That is, the conditions of its actual use to dissuade, deter, and intervene were not explored. Further, the problems created by this policy, and the competitive reactions to it, were not thought through. For instance, to avoid debacles as happened in the 2003 Iraq hunt for weapons of mass destruction, a policy of preemption should be backed up with much stronger intelligence. To initiate a preemptive war, it is reasonable to expect that one would move far beyond secondhand intelligence and demand actual hands-on hard evidence obtained by U.S. forces. Preparing the capability for such a major evidence-producing prestrike operation would have to be a critical objective, yet it was not. Nor was there any evidence that the policy makers had thought through the problem, evident in both the Bosnian and Iraqi interventions, of the United States being fed false or exaggerated intelligence information in order to induce military action to the benefit of an external constituency. Finally, a policy of preemption encourages adversaries to use extreme secrecy, cover parties, and cutouts, and to use, rather than hold, weapons. Policies that anticipated these predictable patterns in others' behavior were lacking. Looking at another section of the national security strategy, I found that the United States will "work with others to defuse regional conflicts." This is an amazingly superficial political slogan. After all, are there really any other alternatives for dealing with regional conflicts? It seems unlikely that the United States could act alone all over the world to defuse regional conflicts, and it seems equally unlikely that we would completely ignore regional conflicts. Stating this slogan provided no useful guidance to anyone. Even worse, it relegated to the status of an annoying detail the fact that this approach was less and less effective. NATO had failed to deliver most of its promised military and development support in Afghanistan, and the United Nations appeared incapable of solving the problems in the Sudan, Uganda, and Nepal, and it appeared to actually foster Israeli-Palestinian conflict. One supposes that the slogan might have been code for "We give up on the United Nations and will work with whoever can help defuse regional conflicts." But a general willingness to work with interested others can hardly be elevated to the status of a "strategy." A strategy would have to explain why regional conflicts, which have been a constant in human activity for millennia, are suddenly a major security problem. And it would have to explain which instruments of U.S. power and influence might be used to convince others to work with the United States on such crusades. It would also have to address the criteria for working with nations that violated the national security strategy's other goals of "human dignity," "free trade," "democracy," and "freedom." As another example of slogans substituted for strategy, consider this keystone goal of the national security strategy: "to prevent our enemies from threatening us, our allies, and our friends, with weapons of mass destruction." Importantly, the 2006 document explained the objective this way: "We aim to convince our adversaries that they cannot achieve their goals with WMD, and thus deter and dissuade them from attempting to use or even acquire these weapons in the first place." It is difficult to understand what the author of this passage had in mind. What would "convince" enemies of the United States that threats based on WMDs would not advance their goals? America's own Cold War strategy had been based on threats to use WMD, which should be convincing evidence that such threats work quite well. It is clear, for instance, that had Saddam Hussein possessed nuclear weapons and the will to use them against allied military forces encamped in Saudi Arabia in

1991, or in Kuwait in 2003, his country would not have been invaded. His threat to kill our soldiers would have been credible, whereas a reciprocal threat to mass murder Iraqi civilians would have been less credible. Russian intelligence officers reported that he understood this logic very well in 1991 and was frustrated that his then-secret nuclear project was not further along. Since the 2006 National Security Strategy does not explain how the deadly effectiveness of nuclear threat is to be mitigated, this particular "goal" appears to be wishful thinking. A logical reaction to these documents' weaknesses might be that they were public—that the real strategies were concealed. I had to reject this explanation. Other analysts with access to privileged information had also called out the lack of substance and coherence in U.S. national strategy. Furthermore, the participants at the CSBA conference were insiders, people who had shaped national policy at the highest levels, and among them there was no disagreement with the assessment that recent attempts at national security strategy had produced a plentitude of vague aspirations and new funding for existing institutions, but no policies or programs that could reasonably be expected to make a difference. My role at the seminar was to provide a business and corporate strategy perspective on these issues. My impression was that the participants anticipated that I would say that business and corporate strategy was done seriously and with growing competence. Using words and slides, I told the group that many businesses did have powerful, effective strategies. But in my personal experiences with corporate practice, both as a consultant and as a field researcher, I saw a growing profusion of what I termed "bad strategy." Bad strategy, I explained, is not the same thing as no strategy or strategy that fails rather than succeeds. Rather, it is an identifiable way of thinking and writing about strategy that has, unfortunately, been gaining ground. Bad strategy is long on goals and short on policy or action. It assumes that goals are all you need. It puts forward strategic objectives that are incoherent and, sometimes, totally impracticable. It uses high-sounding words and phrases to hide these failings. In the several years since that seminar, I have had the opportunity to discuss the bad strategy concept with a number of senior executives. In the process, I have condensed my list of its key hallmarks to the four listed in the beginning of this chapter: fluff, the failure to face the challenge, mistaking goals for strategy, and bad strategic objectives.

Fluff is superficial restatement of the obvious combined with a generous sprinkling of buzzwords. Fluff masquerades as expertise, thought, and analysis. As a simple example of fluff in strategy work, here is a quote from a major retail bank's internal strategy memoranda: "Our fundamental strategy is one of customer-centric intermediation." The Sunday word "intermediation" means that the company accepts deposits and then lends them to others. In other words, it is a bank. The buzz phrase "customer-centric" could mean that the bank competes by offering depositors and lenders better terms or better service. But an examination of its policies and products does not reveal any distinction in this regard. The phrase "customer-centric intermediation" is pure fluff. Pull off the fluffy covering and you have the superficial statement "Our bank's fundamental strategy is being a bank." Fluff has its origins in the academic world and, more recently, in the information technology industry. There, for example, a recent EU report defines "cloud computing" as "an elastic execution environment of resources involving multiple stakeholders and providing a metered service at multiple granularities for a specified level of quality-of-service." 5 A less fluffy explanation is that when you do a Google search, or send data to an Internet backup service, you do not know or care which physical computer, data server, or software system is being used—there is a "cloud" of machines and networks, and it is up to the external service provider to work out how the job is performed and how you will be charged. I saw an example of prime fluff in a summer 2000 presentation by the now-defunct Arthur Andersen. At that moment Enron was a darling of Wall Street, and Arthur Andersen, its auditor, was busy trying to attract new clients based on its knowledge of Enron's business strategy. (This was a presentation by a unit of the Arthur Andersen accounting firm, not by the firm's true consulting arm, Andersen Consulting.) The session was titled "Strategies of the Movers and Shakers." 6 The presenter made it clear that the key "mover and shaker" was Enron, and the excitement was about its recent announcement that it would create a market for trading bandwidth. In the words of the speaker, "Nine months ago, when Enron first announced its bandwidth trading strategy, its market value jumped by $9 billion. Today, the market is valuing the bandwidth trading business at about $30 billion." Deregulation in gas and electricity had created price volatility in these markets. Public utilities, however, preferred stable prices for their inputs. Enron's strategy in the gas and electricity businesses had been to own some physical assets and engage in "basis trading." That is, it would sell a utility a contract for future delivery of gas or electricity at a fixed price and then try to cover that commitment with a mixture of its own supplies and futures contracts. It used a barrage of contracts with speculators and other traders to hedge weather, price, and other risks. By being the dominant player in both gas and electricity trading, it was able to capture information about supplies, demand, and congestion that gave it an edge in its trading activities. The question that should have been on everyone's mind was whether Enron could actually replicate this way of doing business in bandwidth trading. There was no spot price in bandwidth to use for basis trading. There was no standard of quality to help define the deliverable. There was no way to ship bandwidth around to balance supply and demand across geographies. Enron wanted every trader to deal directly with it—the company would not be a middleman—yet its own network node in New York City was some distance from the node used by almost everyone else. And, unlike gas and electricity, the incremental cost of a unit of bandwidth was zero. That meant as long as capacity exceeded demand, the spot price in such a market would be close to zero. Furthermore, by the summer of 2000, it was becoming clear that installed fiber-optic capacity greatly exceeded demand. Finally, in gas and electricity, Enron traded the deliverable, not capacity. But bandwidth was capacity, not the content being delivered. Enron did not have a position in supplying content—online movies and other bandwidth-intensive content were hardly commodities. The argument given at the presentation was that commodity markets "evolve" in the same way, so the same business strategies apply to all. This theory was summarized with the following diagram, a page taken from the PowerPoint handouts at this presentation. This diagram seemed to be describing some sort of "evolution" in these markets from physical delivery toward a "knowledge space" and "exotics." There was the implication that derivative securities (bets on prices) were a means of "sophisticated value extraction." Rather than address the real challenges of establishing a market for bandwidth, this diagram and the accompanying verbal presentation were pure fluff. There was the surface appearance of being analytical and summing up a great deal of information. But a closer examination revealed that it was a stew of half-truths, complex drawings, and buzzwords. IN TODAY'S BANDWIDTH MARKETS, CONNECTIVITYIS KEY Markets do not necessarily evolve from "simple" to "complex"—it often goes the other way around. Yes, you need a basis to create futures and options, but a basis does not have to be a commodity or even a price. Traders, for example, write futures contracts on the Chicago Board Options Exchange Volatility Index (VIX), which is a created measure of price volatility. Yes, Enron's gas and electricity trading were developed out of the ownership of physical assets, but that might be a temporary phenomenon. The oil and agriculture industries had long supported futures contracts and options without heavy participation by producers. Waiting for answers to my questions, I was disappointed. The "meat" in the presentation was the above fluffy diagram and a listing of the new "strategies of the market enablers." The "strategies" mentioned were having an electronic trading platform, being an over-the-counter broker, and being an information provider. These were not strategies—they were just names, like butcher, baker, and candlestick maker. If you accept that the phrase "information provider" describes a business strategy, then you are a prime customer for this sort of fluff. Fourteen months later, it became evident that Enron was failing. With the company's mountain of debt, falling profit margins, failed major projects in the United Kingdom and Brazil, and huge losses in bandwidth trading, outsiders began to doubt its ability to fulfill its side of its contracts. No one wants to write a futures contract with a firm that may fail—which ensures that the firm will fail. As it went bankrupt in December 2001, evidence accumulated about fraudulent accounting practices. The scandal took its auditor, Arthur Andersen, down as well. (The accountant's consulting arm, Andersen Consulting, was renamed Accenture.) A systematic market for trading bandwidth has yet to develop. A hallmark of true expertise and insight is making a complex subject understandable. A hallmark of mediocrity and bad strategy is unnecessary complexity—a flurry of fluff masking an absence of substance. FAILURE TO FACE THE PROBLEM A strategy is a way through a difficulty, an approach to overcoming an obstacle, a response to a challenge. If the challenge is not defined, it is difficult or impossible to assess the quality of the strategy. And if you cannot assess a strategy's quality, you cannot reject a bad strategy or improve a good one. International Harvester was once the fourth largest corporation in the United States. Its roots lay in Cyrus McCormick's reaper, a machine that, together with the railroad, had developed the American plains. In 1977, Harvester's board brought in a new CEO, Archie McCardell, who had been president of Xerox. The board gave him a mandate to turn around the sleepy company. McCardell's administration was the culmination of a decade of modernization. The consulting firm Booz Allen Hamilton had redesigned the organization; Hay Associates had put in modern managerial job descriptions and incentives. McCardell brought with him a new cadre of financial and strategic planners. In July 1979, they produced a thick sheaf of paper titled "Corporate Strategic Plan." It was classic bad strategy. Harvester's corporate strategic plan was an amalgam of five separate strategic plans, each created by one of the operating divisions—agricultural equipment ($3 billion), truck making ($4 billion), industrial equipment ($1 billion), gas turbines ($0.3 billion), and components ($1 billion). The overall "strategy" was to increase the company's market share in each market, cut costs in each business, and thereby ramp up revenue and profit. A summary page from that confidential plan is reproduced on the next page. The graph showing past and forecast profit forms an almost perfect "hockey stick," with an immediate recovery from decline followed by a steady rise. The strategic plan did not lack for texture and detail. Looking within the agricultural equipment group, for example, there is information and discussion about each segment. The overall intent was to strengthen the dealer/distributor network and to reduce manufacturing costs. Market share in agricultural equipment was projected to increase from 16 percent to 20 percent against competitors John Deere, Ford, Massey Ferguson, and J. I. Case. IH CORPORATE SALES, ASSETS & PROFIT BEFORE TAX 1977–1984 The problem with all this was that it ignored the elephant in the elevator. You can't discern the elephant by studying the plan because the plan doesn't mention it. The elephant was Harvester's grossly inefficient work organization, a problem that would not be solved by investing in new equipment or by pressing managers to grow market share. Work rules at Harvester plants, for instance, allowed those with seniority to transfer jobs at will, each transfer setting in motion a cascade of other transfers. As a result, Harvester's profit margin had been about one-half of its competitors' for a long time. In addition, Harvester had the worst labor relations in American industry. It had been the nexus of some of the earliest labor disputes in the United States, especially the 1886 Haymarket riot in Chicago, when an anarchist's bomb killed police and workers at a rally. If you fail to identify and analyze the obstacles, you don't have a strategy. Instead, you have either a stretch goal, a budget, or a list of things you wish would happen. McCardell did improve Harvester's reported profits for a year or two by cutting administrative overhead. But he then forced the company to endure a six-month strike in an attempt to obtain a better union contract. He failed to gain any significant concessions and, after the strike ended, the company quickly began to collapse. During the whole 1979–85 period, it lost more than $3 billion, closed thirty-five of its forty-two plants, and shed eighty-five thousand workers, leaving only fifteen thousand in employment. The company sold off its various businesses, the agricultural equipment going to Tenneco, to merge with its J. I. Case division. The truck division was renamed Navistar and has survived. It is, today, a leading maker of heavy trucks and engines. Today, Harvester's 1979-style strategic planning is out of fashion. Instead of long tables of numbers and bubble charts, we have a different type of ritualized formalism for producing "strategic plans." The current fill-in-the-blanks template starts with a statement of "vision," then a "mission statement" or a list of "core values," then a list of "strategic goals," then for each goal a list of "strategies," and then, finally, a list of "initiatives." (Template-style strategy is explored further in chapter 4, "Why So Much Bad Strategy?") Despite the fact that they are adorned with modern phrases and slogans, most of these strategic plans are as bad as International Harvester's. Like Harvester's, they do not identify and come to grips with the fundamental obstacles and problems that stand in the organization's way. Looking at most of this product, or listening to the managers who have produced it, you will find an almost total lack of strategic thinking. Instead, you will find high-sounding sentiments together with plans to spend more and somehow "get better."

The Defense Advanced Research Projects Agency (DARPA) works to achieve radical technological innovation to support national security. As a counterpoint to Harvester, DARPA's strategy is based on a clear-sighted recognition of the nature of the challenge. Here is DARPA's own statement of a fundamental problem its strategy addresses: A basic challenge for any military research organization is matching military problems with technological opportunities, including the new operational concepts those technologies make possible. Parts of this challenge are extremely difficult because: (1) some military problems have no easy or obvious technical solutions; and (2) some emerging technologies may have farreaching military consequences that are still unclear. DARPA focuses its investments on this "DARPA-hard" niche—a set of technical challenges that, if solved, will be of enormous benefit to U.S. national security, even if the risk of technical failure is high. 7 To attack this challenge, DARPA focuses on projects the military services see as too risky or too removed from their current missions. It tries to imagine what commanders will want in the future rather than what they are calling for today, but it restricts its work to that conducted by very talented people with very good ideas. Some of DARPA's successes include ballistic missile defense, stealth technology,

GPS, speech recognition, the Internet, unmanned land and air vehicles, and nanotechnology. DARPA's strategy is more than a general direction. It includes specific policies that guide its everyday actions. For example, it retains program managers for only four to six years to limit empire building and to bring in fresh talent. The expectation is that a new program manager will be willing to challenge the ideas and work of predecessors. In addition, DARPA has a very limited investment in overhead and physical facilities in order to prevent entrenched interests from thwarting progress in new directions. These policies are based on a realistic appraisal of the obstacles to innovation. They are a far cry from vague aspirations such as "retain the best talent" and "maintain a culture of innovation." DARPA's surprising strategy has a shape and structure common to all good strategy. It follows from a careful definition of the challenge. It anticipates the real-world difficulties to be overcome. It eschews fluff. It creates policies that concentrate resources and actions on surmounting those difficulties. MISTAKING GOALS FOR STRATEGY Chad Logan, the CEO of a graphics arts company, introduced himself to me after hearing a talk I gave on self-control and commitment. He asked me to work with his management team on "strategic thinking." With offices in a downtown commercial building, Logan's company provided custom graphics services to magazines, book publishers, advertisers, and corporations. Logan was a college sports hero turned graphics artist who had moved into sales. He was also the nephew of the founder; when the founder died two years before, Logan became the company's principle owner. The edge-of-town offices and work spaces were utilitarian; the CEO's conference room was paneled in teak. Brightly lighted examples of the company's work hung on the walls and reflected from the surface of the polished conference table. The business was organized into a large design group and three sales departments: Media sold to magazines and newspapers, Corporate sold to corporations for catalogs and brochures, and Digital sold mainly to Web-based customers. Logan explained that his overall goal was simple—he called it the "20/20" plan. Revenues were to grow at 20 percent per year and the profit margin was to be 20 percent or higher. "Our overall strategy is set," he said. "We are going to grow, and grow profitably. My problem is getting everyone aligned for this push. What I need is some coaching for my top people. I want them to be totally up to speed on strategic thinking. I want skills they can use tomorrow in a meeting with a client." I asked Logan if he had worked out any elements of his strategy other than the growth and margin goals. He slid a document across the tabletop. It was titled "2005 Strategic Plan." Mostly, it was a set of projections: revenues, costs, gross profit, and so on. The projections went out four years. In the previous four or five years, the company had held its market share and its after-tax profit margin had been about 12 percent, which is typical for this industry. The projections were based on a 20 percent profit margin and 20 percent per year revenue growth. The first page of the document was labeled "Our Key Strategies:" OUR KEY STRATEGIES • We will be the graphics arts services firm of choice. • We will delight our customers with unique and creative solutions to their problems. • We will grow revenue by at least 20% each year. • We will maintain a profit margin of at least 20%. • We will have a culture of commitment. Corporate goals are commitments we all work to keep. • We will foster an honest and open work environment. • We will work to support the broader community in which we operate. "We spent about three weeks, going around to everyone, to develop these key strategies," said Logan. "I believe in them. I believe that we can have a company that we are each proud to be part of and that is worth the effort it takes to win. There is very good buy-in on these key strategies." "This 20/20 plan is a very aggressive financial goal," I said. "What has to happen for it to be realized?" Logan tapped the plan with a blunt forefinger. "The thing I learned as a football player is that winning requires strength and skill, but more than anything it requires the will to win—the drive to succeed. The managers and staff in this company have worked hard, and the transition to digital technologies was handled well. But there is a difference between working hard and having your eye on the prize and the will to win. Sure, 20/20 is a stretch, but the secret of success is setting your sights high. We are going to get moving and keep pushing until we get there." When I asked Logan "What has to happen?" I was looking for some point of leverage, some reason to believe this fairly quiet company could explode with growth and profit. A strategy is like a lever that magnifies force. Yes, you might be able to drag a giant block of rock across the ground with muscles, ropes, and motivation. But it is wiser to build levers and wheels and then move the rock. I tried again: "Chad, when a company makes the kind of jump in performance your plan envisions, there is usually a key strength you are building on or a change in the industry that opens up new opportunities. Can you clarify what the point of leverage might be here, in your company?" Logan frowned and pressed his lips together, expressing frustration that I didn't understand his meaning. He pulled a sheet of paper out of his briefcase and ran a finger under the highlighted text. "This is what Jack Welch says," he told me. The text read: "We have found that by reaching for what appears to be the impossible, we often actually do the impossible." "That's what we are going to do here," said Logan. I didn't think that Logan's concept of his 20/20 goal was a useful way to proceed. Strategic objectives should address a specific process or accomplishment, such as halving the time it takes to respond to a customer, or getting work from several Fortune 500 corporations. However, arguing with him at that juncture wouldn't have been productive. A client has to first agree to engage in a dialogue before a tough back-and-forth can be productive. "All right," I said. "I see where you are coming from. Give me some time to look over these numbers." In truth, I didn't really need to study the numbers. What I needed was some time to think about my own approach to helping Logan. Although he was well-intentioned, his plan, to me, was all results and no action. In his own mind, he believed in courage, boldness, motivation, and push. His reference to "pushing until we get there" triggered, in my mind, an association with the great pushes of 1915–17 during World War I, especially at Passchendaele. When war broke out in 1914, jubilant crowds jammed the streets of cities, and young men hurled hats in the air as they marched off to prove themselves. The philosophy of the age, most fervently adopted by the French, was that willpower, spirit, morale, élan, and aggressiveness were the keys to success. For three years, generals flung highly motivated men at fortified machine-gun emplacements, only to see tens of thousands, then hundreds of thousands, shredded to mincemeat to gain a mile of useless ground. In 1917, around the village of Passchendaele in Flanders, British general Douglas Haig planned an assault. He wanted to break through the Germans' fortified lines and open up a path to the sea, dividing the German army. He had been advised that shelling the German fortified positions would destroy the dikes and flood the below-sea-level fields. He shelled the German fortifications anyway. The shelling broke the dikes and churned the rich soil to sticky yellow clay, a quagmire that men sank into up to their knees and bellies. It drowned tanks, horses, and the wounded. Haig, stung by the death of 100,000 British troops at the Somme a year earlier, had promised to call off the advance if it did not go well. It didn't, yet the doctrine of motivation and "one last push" continued for three months, despite appalling losses. In a final ten-day assault, Canadian troops pressed directly into the machine-gun fire, floundering in the mud and body parts of comrades; they suffered 16,000 casualties to take a small hill. Over the three months of battle, five miles of ground were gained and more than 70,000 Allied soldiers died in the muck. Another 250,000 were wounded. Winston Churchill described Passchendaele as "a forlorn expenditure of valour and life without equal in futility." At the Somme and Passchendaele, Haig led an entire generation of British and Dominion youth to their deaths—as Joseph Joffre did for the French at the Somme, and Erich von Falkenhayn did for the Germans at Verdun. In Europe, motivational speakers are not the staple on the management lecture circuit that they are in the United States, where the doctrine of leadership as motivation is alive and well. Here, for example, is H. Ross Perot: "Most people give up just when they're about to achieve success. They quit on the one-yard line. They give up at the last minute of the game, one foot from a winning touchdown." Hearing this, many Americans nod in agreement. Many Europeans, by contrast, hear the echo of the "one last push" at Passchendaele. There, the slaughtered troops did not suffer from a lack of motivation. They suffered from a lack of competent strategic leadership. Motivation is an essential part of life and success, and a leader may justly ask for "one last push," but the leader's job is more than that. The job of the leader is also to create the conditions that will make that push effective, to have a strategy worthy of the effort called upon.I think you have a lot of ambition, but you don't have a strategy. I don't think it would be useful, right now, to work with your managers on strategies for meeting the 20/20 goal. What I would advise is that you first work to discover the very most promising opportunities for the business. Those opportunities may be internal, fixing bottlenecks and constraints in the way people work, or external. To do this, you should probably pull together a small team of people and take a month to do a review of who your buyers are, who you compete with, and what opportunities exist. It's normally a good idea to look very closely at what is changing in your business, where you might get a jump on the competition. You should open things up so there are as many useful bits of information on the table as possible. If you want, I can help you structure some of this process and, maybe, help you ask some of the right questions. The end result will be a strategy that is aimed at channeling energy into what seem to be one or two of the most attractive opportunities, where it looks like you can make major inroads or breakthroughs. I can't tell you in advance how large such opportunities are, or where they may be. I can't tell you in advance how fast revenues will grow. Perhaps you will want to add new services, or cut back on doing certain things that don't make a profit. Perhaps you will find it more promising to focus on grabbing the graphics work that currently goes in-house, rather than to competitors. But, in the end, you should have a very short list of the most important things for the company to do. Then you will have a basis for moving forward. That is what I would do were I in your shoes. If you continue down the road you are on you will be counting on motivation to move the company forward. I cannot honestly recommend that as a way forward because business competition is not just a battle of strength and wills; it is also a competition over insights and competencies. My judgment is that motivation, by itself, will not give this company enough of an edge to achieve your goals. Chad Logan thanked me and, a week later, retained someone else to help him. The new consultant took Logan and his department managers through an exercise he called "Visioning." The gist of it was the question "How big do you think this company can be?" In the morning they stretched their aspirations from "bigger" to "very much bigger." Then, in the afternoon, the facilitator challenged them to an even grander vision: "Think twice as big as that," he pressed. Logan was pleased. I was pleased to be elsewhere engaged. Chad Logan's "key strategies" had little to do with strategy. They were simply performance goals. This same problem affects many corporate "strategy plans." Business leaders know their organizations should have a strategy. Yet many express frustration with the whole process of strategic planning. The reason for this dissatisfaction is that most corporate strategic plans are simply three-year or five-year rolling budgets combined with market share projections. Calling a rolling budget of this type a "strategic plan" gives people false expectations that the exercise will somehow result in a coherent strategy. There is nothing wrong with planning. It is an essential part of management. Take, for example, a rapidly growing retail chain. It needs a plan to guide property acquisition, construction, training, and so on. This is what a resource plan does—it makes sure resources arrive when they are needed and helps management detect surprises. Similarly, a multinational engineering company needs a plan to guide and fit together its human resource activities, the opening and expansion of offices in various regions, and its financing policies. You can call these annual exercises "strategic planning" if you like, but they are not strategy. They cannot deliver what senior managers want: a pathway to substantially higher performance. To obtain higher performance, leaders must identify the critical obstacles to forward progress and then develop a coherent approach to overcoming them. This may require product innovation, or new approaches to distribution, or a change in organizational structure. Or it may exploit insights into the implications of changes in the environment—in technology, consumer tastes, laws, resource prices, or competitive behavior. The leader's responsibility is to decide which of these pathways will be the most fruitful and design a way to marshal the organization's knowledge, resources, and energy to that end. Importantly, opportunities, challenges, and changes don't come along in nice annual packages. The need for true strategy work is episodic, not necessarily annual. BAD STRATEGIC OBJECTIVES If you are a midlevel manager, your boss sets your goals. Or, if you work in an enlightened company, you and your boss negotiate over your goals. In either setting, it is natural to think of strategies as actions designed to accomplish specific goals. However, taking this way of thinking into a top-level position is a mistake. Being a general manager, CEO, president, or other top-level leader means having more power and being less constrained. Effective senior leaders don't chase arbitrary goals. Rather, they decide which general goals should be pursued. And they design the subgoals that various pieces of the organization work toward. Indeed, the cutting edge of any strategy is the set of strategic objectives (subgoals) it lays out. One of the challenges of being a leader is mastering this shift from having others define your goals to being the architect of the organization's purposes and objectives. To help clarify this distinction it is helpful to use the word "goal" to express overall values and desires and to use the word "objective" to denote specific operational targets. Thus, the United States may have "goals" of freedom, justice, peace, security, and happiness. It is strategy which transforms these vague overall goals into a coherent set of actionable objectives—defeat the Taliban and rebuild a decaying infrastructure. A leader's most important job is creating and constantly adjusting this strategic bridge between goals and objectives. For example, Chen Brothers was a rapidly growing regional distributor of specialty foods. Its overall goals included growing profit, being a good place to work, and being seen as the go-to distributor for organic foods. These were all worthy goals. None of them, however, implied a particular strategy or action, although they can be seen as constraints (that is, these sorts of broad "goals" work like the rules of football in that they rule out a great many actions without specifying what the team should actually do). Chen Brothers'strategy had been to target local specialty retailers that would pay a price premium to carry distinctive products not available at the large chain stores. Top management had divided its customers and potential customers into three tiers and set strategic objectives for each tier. The most important objectives were shelf-space dominance in the top tier, promotional parity or better in the middle tier, and growing penetration in the lowest tier. The recent rapid growth of Whole Foods was putting increasing pressure on the local specialty shops that had been Chen Brothers' target market. Accordingly, management was formulating a new strategy of linking together small local food producers under a common brand that could be sold through Whole Foods. This change in strategy had no impact on the company's overall goals, but clearly meant a radical restructuring of its current strategic objectives. Instead of penetration objectives for different classes of retailers, Chen Brothers put together a "Whole Foods" team that combined production, marketing, advertising, distribution, and financial expertise. The team was entirely focused on the objective of making Chen Brothers' most distinctive new product a national account at Whole Foods. Once that was accomplished, further objectives concerning other products, shelf space, and market share would be set. Chen Brothers did not fall into the trap of believing that strategy is a grand vision or a set of financial goals. Instead, management had skillfully designed a "way forward" that concentrated corporate attention on one or two important objectives. Once accomplished, new opportunities would open up and more ambitious objectives could be set. Dog's Dinner Objectives Good strategy works by focusing energy and resources on one, or a very few, pivotal objectives whose accomplishment will lead to a cascade of favorable outcomes. One form of bad strategic objectives occurs when there is a scrambled mess of things to accomplish—a "dog's dinner" of strategic objectives. A long list of "things to do," often mislabeled as "strategies" or "objectives," is not a strategy. It is just a list of things to do. Such lists usually grow out of planning meetings in which a wide variety of stakeholders make suggestions as to things they would like to see done. Rather than focus on a few important items, the group sweeps the whole day's collection into the "strategic plan." Then, in recognition that it is a dog's dinner, the label "long-term" is added so that none of them need be done today. As a vivid example, I recently had the chance to discuss strategy with the mayor of a small city in the Pacific Northwest. His planning committee's strategic plan contained 47 "strategies" and 178 action items. Action item number 122 was to "create a strategic plan." As another example, the Los Angeles Unified School District's strategic plan for "high-priority schools" (discussed on the next page) contained 7 "strategies," 26 "tactics," and 234 "action steps," a true dog's dinner of things to do. This pattern is all too common in city, school district, and nonprofit strategy work, as well as in some business firms.

CHAPTER SIX

Reconstruct Market Boundaries

THE FIR ST PRI NCIPLE of blue ocean strategy is to reconstruct market boundaries to break from the competition and create blue oceans. This principle addresses the search risk many companies struggle with. The challenge is to successfully identify, out of the haystack of possibilities that exist, commercially compelling blue ocean opportunities. This challenge is key because managers cannot afford to be riverboat gamblers betting their strategy on intuition or on a random drawing. In conducting our research, we sought to discover whether there were systematic patterns for reconstructing market boundaries to create blue oceans. And, if there were, we wanted to know whether these patterns applied across all types of industry sectors—from consumer goods, to industrial products, to finance and services, to telecoms and IT, to pharmaceuticals and B2B—or were they limited to specific industries? We found clear patterns for creating blue oceans. Specifically, we found six basic approaches to remaking market boundaries. We call this the six paths framework. These paths have general applicability across industry sectors, and they lead companies into the corridor of commercially viable blue ocean ideas. None of these paths requires special vision or foresight about the future. All are based on looking at familiar data from a new perspective. These paths challenge the six fundamental assumptions underlying many companies' strategies. These six assumptions, on which most companies hypnotically build their strategies, keep companies trapped competing in red oceans. Specifically, companies tend to do the following: • Define their industry similarly and focus on being the best within it • Look at their industries through the lens of generally accepted strategic groups (such as luxury automobiles, economy cars, and family vehicles), and strive to stand out in the strategic group they play in • Focus on the same buyer group, be it the purchaser (as in the office equipment industry), the user (as in the clothing industry), or the influencer (as in the pharmaceutical industry) • Define the scope of the products and services offered by their industry similarly • Accept their industry's functional or emotional orientation • Focus on the same point in time—and often on current competitive threats—in formulating strategy The more that companies share this conventional wisdom about how they compete, the greater the competitive convergence among them. To break out of red oceans, companies must break out of the accepted boundaries that define how they compete. Instead of looking within these boundaries, managers need to look systematically across them to create blue oceans. They need to look across alternative industries, across strategic groups, across buyer groups, across complementary product and service offerings, across thefunctional-emotional orientation of an industry, and even across time. This gives companies keen insight into how to reconstruct market realities to open up blue oceans. Let's examine how each of these six paths works. Path 1: Look Across Alternative Industries In the broadest sense, a company competes not only with the other firms in its own industry but also with companies in those other industries that produce alternative products or services. Alternatives are broader than substitutes. Products or services that have different forms but offer the same functionality or core utility are often substitutes for each other. On the other hand, alternatives include products or services that have different functions and forms but the same purpose. For example, to sort out their personal finances, people can buy and install a financial software package, hire a CPA, or simply use pencil and paper. The software, the CPA, and the pencil are largely substitutes for each other. They have very different forms but serve the same function: helping people manage their financial affairs. In contrast, products or services can take different forms and perform different functions but serve the same objective. Consider cinemas versus restaurants. Restaurants have few physical features in common with cinemas and serve a distinct function: They provide conversational and gastronomical pleasure. This is a very different experience from the visual entertainment offered by cinemas. Despite the differences in form and function, however, people go to a restaurant for the same objective that they go to the movies: to enjoy a night out. These are not substitutes, but alternatives to choose from. In making every purchase decision, buyers implicitly weigh alternatives, often unconsciously. Do you need a self-indulgent two hours? What should you do to achieve it? Do you go to movie, have a massage, or enjoy reading a favorite book at a local café? The thought process is intuitive for individual consumers and industrial buyers alike. For some reason, we often abandon this intuitive thinking when we become sellers. Rarely do sellers think consciously about how their customers make trade-offs across alternative industries. A shift in price, a change in model, even a new ad campaign can elicit a tremendous response from rivals within an industry, but the same actions in an alternative industry usually go unnoticed. Trade journals, trade shows, and consumer rating reports reinforce the vertical walls between one industry and another. Often, however, the space between alternative industries provides opportunities for value innovation. Consider NetJets, which created the blue ocean of fractional jet ownership. In less than twenty years NetJets has grown larger than many airlines, with more than five hundred aircraft, operating more than two hundred fifty thousand flights to more than one hundred forty countries. Purchased by Berkshire Hathaway in 1998, today NetJets is a multibillion-dollar business, with revenues growing at 30–35 percent per year from 1993 to 2000. NetJets' success has been attributed to its flexibility, shortened travel time, hasslefree travel experience, increased reliability, and strategic pricing. The reality is that NetJets reconstructed market boundaries to create this blue ocean by looking across alternative industries. The most lucrative mass of customers in the aviation industry are corporate travelers. NetJets looked at the existing alternatives and found that when business travelers want to fly, they have two principal choices. On the one hand, a company's executives can fly business class or first class on a commercial airline. On the other hand, a company can purchase its own aircraft to serve its corporate travel needs. The strategic question is, Why would corporations choose one alternative industry over another? By focusing on the key factors that lead corporations to trade across alternatives and eliminating or reducing everything else, NetJets created its blue ocean strategy. Consider this: Why do corporations choose to use commercial airlines for their corporate travel? Surely it's not because of the long check-in and security lines, hectic flight transfers, overnight stays, or congested airports. Rather, they choose commercial airlines for only one reason: costs. On the one hand, commercial travel avoids the high up-front, fixed-cost investment of a multimilliondollar jet aircraft. On the other hand, a company purchases only the number of corporate airline tickets needed per year, lowering variable costs and reducing the possibility of unused aviation travel time that often accompanies the ownership of corporate jets. So NetJets offers its customers one-sixteenth ownership of an aircraft to be shared with fifteen other customers, each one entitled to fifty hours of flight time per year. Starting at $375,000 (plus pilot, maintenance, and other monthly costs), owners can purchase a share in a $6 million aircraft.1 Customers get the convenience of a private jet at the price of a commercial airline ticket. Comparing first-class travel with private aircraft, the National Business Aviation Association found that when direct and indirect costs—hotel, meals, travel time, expenses—were factored in, the cost of firstclass commercial travel was significantly higher. In a cost-benefit analysis for four passengers on a theoretical trip from Newark to Austin, the real cost of the commercial trip was $19,400, compared with $10,100 in a private jet.2 As for NetJets, it avoids the enormous fixed costs that commercial airlines attempt to cover by filling larger and larger aircraft. NetJets' smaller airplanes, the use of smaller regional airports, and limited staff keep costs to a minimum. To understand the rest of the NetJets formula, consider the flip side: Why do people choose corporate jets over commercial travel? Certainly it is not to pay the multimillion-dollar price to purchase planes. Nor is it to set up a dedicated flight department to take care of scheduling and other administrative matters. Nor it is to pay socalled deadhead costs—the costs of flying the aircraft from its home base to where it is needed. Rather, corporations buy private jets to dramatically cut total travel time, to reduce the hassle of congested airports, to allow for point-to-point travel, and to gain the benefit of having more productive and energized executives who can hit the ground running upon arrival. So NetJets built on these distinctive strengths. Whereas 70 percent of commercial flights went to only thirty airports across the United States, NetJets offered access to more than five thousand five hundred airports across the country, in convenient locations near business centers. On international flights, your plane pulls directly up to the customs office. With point-to-point service and the exponential increase in the number of airports to land in, there are no flight transfers; trips that would otherwise require overnight stays can be completed in a single day. The time from your car to takeoff is measured in minutes instead of hours. For example, whereas a flight from Washington, D.C., to Sacramento would take 10.5 hours on a commercial airline, it is only 5.2 hours on a NetJets aircraft; from Palm Springs to Cabo San Lucas takes 6 hours commercial, and only 2.1 hours via NetJets.3 NetJets offers substantial cost savings in total travel time. Perhaps most appealing, your jet is always available with only four hours' notice. If a jet is not available, NetJets will charter one for you. Last but not least, NetJets dramatically reduces issues related to security threats and offers clients customized in-flight service, such as having your favorite food and beverages ready for you when you board. By offering the best of commercial travel and private jets and eliminating and reducing everything else, NetJets opened up a multibillion-dollar blue ocean wherein customers get the convenience and speed of a private jet with a low fixed cost and the low variable cost of commercial airline travel (see figure 3-1). And the competition? According to NetJets, in the past seven years fiftyseven companies have set up fractional jet operations; of those, fifty-seven have gone out of business. The biggest telecommunications success in Japan since the 1980s also has its roots in path 1. Here we are speaking of NTT DoCoMo's i-mode, which was launched in 1999. The i-mode service changed the way people communicate and access information in Japan. NTT DoCoMo's insight into creating a blue ocean came by thinking about why people trade-across the alternatives of mobile phones and the Internet. With deregulation of the Japanese telecommunications industry, new competitors were entering the market and price competition and technological races were the norm. The result was that costs were rising while the average revenue per user fell. NTT DoCoMo broke out of this red ocean of bloody competition by creating a blue ocean of wireless transmission not only of voice but also of text, data, and pictures. NTT DoCoMo asked, What are the distinctive strengths of the Internet over cell phones, and vice versa? Although the Internet offered endless information and services, the killer apps were e-mail, simple information (such as news, weather forecasts, and a telephone directory), and entertainment (including games, events, and music entertainment). The key downside of the Internet was the far higher price of computer hardware, an overload of information, the nuisance of dialing up to go online, and the fear of giving credit card information electronically. On the other hand, the distinctive strengths of mobile phones were their mobility, voice transmission, and ease of use. NTT DoCoMo broke the trade-off between these two alternatives, not by creating new technology but by focusing on the decisive advantages that the Internet has over the cell phone and vice versa. The company eliminated or reduced everything else. Its userfriendly interface has one simple button, the i-mode button (i standing for interactive, Internet, information, and the English pronoun I), which users press to give them immediate access to the few killer apps of the Internet. Instead of barraging you with infinite information as on the Internet, however, the i-mode button acts as a hotel concierge service, connecting only to preselected and preapproved sites for the most popular Internet applications. That makes navigation fast and easy. At the same time, even though the i-mode phone is priced 25 percent higher than a regular cell phone, the price of the i-mode phone is dramatically less than that of a PC, and its mobility is high. Moreover, beyond adding voice, the i-mode uses a simple billing service whereby all the services used on the Web via the i-mode are billed to the user on the same monthly bill. This dramatically reduces the number of bills users receive and eliminates the need to give credit card details, as on the Internet. And because the i-mode service is automatically turned on whenever the phone is on, users are always connected and have no need to go through the hassle of logging on. Neither the standard cell phone nor the PC could compete with i-mode's divergent value curve. By the end of 2003 the number of i-mode subscribers had reached 40.1 million, and revenues from the transmission of data, pictures, and text increased from 295 million yen ($2.6 million) in 1999 to 886.3 billion yen ($8 billion) in 2003. The i-mode service did not simply win customers from competitors. It dramatically grew the market, drawing in youth and senior citizens and converting voice-only customers to voice and data transmission customers.

Ironically, European and U.S. counterparts who have been scrambling to unlock a similar blue ocean in the West have so far failed. Why? Our assessment shows that they have been focused on delivering the most sophisticated technology, WAP (wireless application protocol), instead of delivering exceptional value. This has led them to build overcomplicated offerings that miss the key commonalities valued by the mass of people. Many other well-known success stories have looked across alternatives to create new markets. The Home Depot offers the expertise of professional home contractors at markedly lower prices than hardware stores. By delivering the decisive advantages of both alternative industries—and eliminating or reducing everything else—The Home Depot has transformed enormous latent demand for home improvement into real demand, making ordinary homeowners into do-it-yourselfers. Southwest Airlines concentrated on driving as the alternative to flying, providing the speed of air travel at the price of car travel and creating the blue ocean of short-haul air travel. Similarly, Intuit looked to the pencil as the chief alternative to personal financial software to develop the fun and intuitive Quicken software. What are the alternative industries to your industry? Why do customers trade across them? By focusing on the key factors that lead buyers to trade across alternative industries and eliminating or reducing everything else, you can create a blue ocean of new market space. Path 2: Look Across Strategic Groups Within Industries Just as blue oceans can often be created by looking across alternative industries, so can they be unlocked by looking across strategic groups. The term refers to a group of companies within an industry that pursue a similar strategy. In most industries, the fundamental strategic differences among industry players are captured by a small number of strategic groups. Strategic groups can generally be ranked in a rough hierarchical order built on two dimensions: price and performance. Each jump in price tends to bring a corresponding jump in some dimensions of performance. Most companies focus on improving their competitive position within a strategic group. Mercedes, BMW, and Jaguar, for example, focus on outcompeting one another in the luxury car segment as economy car makers focus on excelling over one another in their strategic group. Neither strategic group, however, pays much heed to what the other is doing because from a supply point of view they do not seem to be competing. The key to creating a blue ocean across existing strategic groups is to break out of this narrow tunnel vision by understanding which factors determine customers' decisions to trade up or down from one group to another. Consider Curves, the Texas-based women's fitness company. Since franchising began in 1995, Curves has grown like wildfire, acquiring more than two million members in more than six thousand locations, with total revenues exceeding the $1 billion mark. A new Curves opens, on average, every four hours somewhere in the world. What's more, this growth was triggered almost entirely through word of mouth and buddy referrals. Yet, at its inception, Curves was seen as entering an oversaturated market, gearing its offering to customers who would not want it, and making its offering significantly blander than the competition's. In reality, however, Curves exploded demand in the U.S. fitness industry, unlocking a huge untapped market, a veritable blue ocean of women struggling and failing to keep in shape through sound fitness. Curves built on the decisive advantages of two strategic groups in the U.S. fitness industry—traditional health clubs and home exercise programs— and eliminated or reduced everything else. At the one extreme, the U.S. fitness industry is awash with traditional health clubs that catered to both men and women, offering a full range of exercise and sporting options, usually in upscale urban locations. Their trendy facilities are designed to attract the high-end health club set. They have the full range of aerobic and strength training machines, a juice bar, instructors, and a full locker room with showers and sauna, because the aim is for customers to spend social as well as exercise time there. Having fought their way across town to health clubs, customers typically spend at least an hour there, and more often two. Membership fees for all this are typically in the range of $100 per month—not cheap, guaranteeing that the market would stay upscale and small. Traditional health club customers represent only 12 percent of the entire population, concentrated overwhelmingly in the larger urban areas. Investment costs for a traditional full-service health club run from $500,000 to more than $1 million, depending on the city center location. At the other extreme is the strategic group of home exercise programs, such as exercise videos, books, and magazines. These are a small fraction of the cost, are used at home, and generally require little or no exercise equipment. Instruction is minimal, being confined to the star of the exercise video or book and magazine explanations and illustrations. The question is, What makes women trade either up or down between traditional health clubs and home exercise programs? Most women don't trade up to health clubs for the profusion of special machines, juice bars, locker rooms with sauna, pool, and the chance to meet men. The average female nonathlete does not even want to run into men when she is working out, perhaps revealing lumps in her leotards. She is not inspired to line up behind machines in which she needs to change weights and adjust their incline angles. As for time, it has become an increasingly scarce commodity for the average woman. Few can afford to spend one to two hours at a health club several times a week. For the mass of women, the city center locations also present traffic challenges, something that increases stress and discourages going to the gym. It turns out that most women trade up to health clubs for one principal reason. When they are at home it's too easy to find an excuse for not working out. It is hard to be disciplined in the confines of one's home if you are not already a committed sports enthusiast. Working out collectively, instead of alone, is more motivating and inspiring. Conversely, women who use home exercise programs do so primarily for the time saving, lower costs, and privacy. Curves built its blue ocean by drawing on the distinctive strengths of these two strategic groups, eliminating and reducing everything else.

Curves has eliminated all the aspects of the traditional health club that are of little interest to the broad mass of women. Gone are the profusion of special machines, food, spa, pool, and even locker rooms, which have been replaced by a few curtainedoff changing areas. The experience in a Curves club is entirely different from that in a typical health club. The member enters the exercise room where the machines (typically about ten) are arranged, not in rows facing a television as in the health club, but in a circle to facilitate interchange among members, making the experience fun. The QuickFit circuit training system uses hydraulic exercise machines, which need no adjusting, are safe, simple to use, and nonthreatening. Specifically designed for women, these machines reduce impact stress and build strength and muscle. While exercising, members can talk and support one another, and the social, nonjudgmental atmosphere is totally different from that of a typical health club. There are few if any mirrors on the wall, and there are no men staring at you. Members move around the circle of machines and aerobic pads and in thirty minutes complete the whole workout. The result of reducing and focusing service on the essentials is that prices fall to around $30 per month, opening the market to the broad mass of women. Curves' tagline could be "for the price of a cup of coffee a day you can obtain the gift of health through proper exercise." Curves offers the distinctive value depicted in figure 3-2 at a lower cost. Compared with the start up investment of $500,000 to $1 million for traditional health clubs, start-up investments for Curves are in the range of only $25,000 to $30,000 (excluding a $20,000 franchise fee) because of the wide range of factors the company eliminated. Variable costs are also significantly lower, with personnel and maintenance of facilities dramatically reduced and rent reduced because of the much smaller spaces required: 1,500 square feet in nonprime suburban locations versus 35,000 to 100,000 square feet in prime urban locations. Curves' low-cost business model makes its franchises easy to afford and helps explain why they have mushroomed quickly. Most franchises are profitable within a few months, as soon as they recruit on average one hundred members. Established Curves franchises are selling in the range of $100,000 to $150,000 on the secondary market. The result is that Curves facilities are everywhere in most towns of any size. Curves is not competing directly with other health and exercise concepts; it created new blue ocean demand. As the United States and North America become saturated, management has plans to expand into Europe. Expansion has already begun in Latin America and Spain. By the end of 2004, Curves is expected to reach eight thousand five hundred fitness centers.

Beyond Curves, many companies have created blue oceans by looking across strategic groups. Ralph Lauren created the blue ocean of "high fashion with no fashion." Its designer name, the elegance of its stores, and the luxury of its materials capture what most customers value in haute couture. At the same time, its updated classical look and price capture the best of the classical lines such as Brooks Brothers and Burberry. By combining the most attractive factors of both groups and eliminating or reducing everything else, Polo Ralph Lauren not only captured share from both segments but also drew many new customers into the market. In the luxury car market, Toyota's Lexus carved out a new blue ocean by offering the quality of the high-end Mercedes, BMW, and Jaguar at a price closer to the lower-end Cadillac and Lincoln. And think of the Sony Walkman. By looking across the high fidelity of boom boxes with the low price and mobility of transistor radios within the audio equipment industry, Sony created the personal portable-stereo market in the late 1970s. The Walkman took share from these two strategic groups. In addition, its leap in value drew new customers, including joggers and commuters, into this blue ocean. Michigan-based Champion Enterprises identified a similar opportunity by looking across two strategic groups in the housing industry: makers of prefabricated housing and on-site developers. Prefabricated houses are cheap and quick to build, but they are also dismally standardized and have a low-quality image. Houses built by developers on-site offer variety and an image of high quality but are dramatically more expensive and take longer to build. Champion created a blue ocean by offering the decisive advantages of both strategic groups. Its prefabricated houses are quick to build and benefit from tremendous economies of scale and lower costs, but Champion also allows buyers to choose such high-end finishing touches as fireplaces, skylights, and even vaulted ceilings to give the homes a personal feel. In essence, Champion has changed the definition of prefabricated housing. As a result, far more lowerto middle-income buyers have become interested in purchasing prefabricated housing rather than renting or buying an apartment, and even some affluent people are being drawn into the market. What are the strategic groups in your industry? Why do customers trade up for the higher group, and why do they trade down for the lower one? Path 3: Look Across the Chain of Buyers In most industries, competitors converge around a common definition of who the target buyer is. In reality, though, there is a chain of "buyers" who are directly or indirectly involved in the buying decision. The purchasers who pay for the product or service may differ from the actual users, and in some cases there are important influencers as well. Although these three groups may overlap, they often differ. When they do, they frequently hold different definitions of value. A corporate purchasing agent, for example, may be more concerned with costs than the corporate user, who is likely to be far more concerned with ease of use. Similarly, a retailer may value a manufacturer's just-in-time stock replenishment and innovative financing. But consumer purchasers, although strongly influenced by the channel, do not value these things. Individual companies in an industry often target different customer segments—for example, large versus small customers. But an industry typically converges on a single buyer group. The pharmaceutical industry, for example, focuses overridingly on influencers: doctors. The office equipment industry focuses heavily on purchasers: corporate purchasing departments. And the clothing industry sells predominantly to users. Sometimes there is a strong economic rationale for this focus. But often it is the result of industry practices that have never been questioned. Challenging an industry's conventional wisdom about which buyer group to target can lead to the discovery of new blue ocean. By looking across buyer groups, companies can gain new insights

into how to redesign their value curves to focus on a previously overlooked set of buyers. Think of Novo Nordisk, the Danish insulin producer that created a blue ocean in the insulin industry. Insulin is used by diabetics to regulate the level of sugar in their blood. Historically, the insulin industry, like most of the pharmaceutical industry, focused its attention on the key influencers: doctors. The importance of doctors in affecting the insulin purchasing decision of diabetics made doctors the target buyer group of the industry. Accordingly, the industry geared its attention and efforts to produce purer insulin in response to doctors' quest for better medication. The issue was that innovations in purification technology had improved dramatically by the early 1980s. As long as the purity of insulin was the major parameter upon which companies competed, little progress could be made further in that direction. Novo itself had already created the first "human monocomponent" insulin that was a chemically exact copy of human insulin. Competitive convergence among the major players was rapidly occurring. Novo Nordisk, however, saw that it could break away from the competition and create a blue ocean by shifting the industry's longstanding focus on doctors to the users—patients themselves. In focusing on patients, Novo Nordisk found that insulin, which was supplied to diabetes patients in vials, presented significant challenges in administering. Vials left the patient with the complex and unpleasant task of handling syringes, needles, and insulin, and of administering doses according to his or her needs. Needles and syringes also evoked unpleasant feelings of social stigmatism for patients. And patients did not want to fiddle with syringes and needles outside their homes, a frequent occurrence because many patients must inject insulin several times a day. This led Novo Nordisk to the blue ocean opportunity of NovoPen, launched in 1985. NovoPen, the first user-friendly insulin delivery solution, was designed to remove the hassle and embarrassment of administering insulin. The NovoPen resembled a fountain pen; it contained an insulin cartridge that allowed the patient to easily carry, in one self-contained unit, roughly a week's worth of insulin. The pen had an integrated click mechanism, making it possible for even blind patients to control the dosing and administer insulin. Patients could take the pen with them and inject insulin with ease and convenience without the embarrassing complexity of syringes and needles. To dominate the blue ocean it had unlocked, Novo Nordisk followed up by introducing, in 1989, NovoLet, a prefilled disposable insulin injection pen with a dosing system that provided users with even greater convenience and ease of use. And in 1999 it brought out the Innovo, an integrated electronic memory and cartridgebased delivery system. Innovo was designed to manage the delivery of insulin through built-in memory and to display the dose, the last dose, and the elapsed time—information that is critical for reducing risk and eliminating worries about missing a dose. Novo Nordisk's blue ocean strategy shifted the industry landscape and transformed the company from an insulin producer to a diabetes care company. NovoPen and the later delivery systems swept over the insulin market. Sales of insulin in prefilled devices or pens now account for the dominant share in Europe and Japan, where patients are advised to take frequent injections of insulin every day. Although Novo Nordisk itself has more than a 60 percent share in Europe and 80 percent in Japan, 70 percent of its total turnover comes from diabetes care, an offering that originated largely in the company's thinking in terms of users rather than influencers. Similarly, consider Bloomberg. In a little more than a decade, Bloomberg became one of the largest and most profitable businessinformation providers in the world. Until Bloomberg's debut in the early 1980s, Reuters and Telerate dominated the online financialinformation industry, providing news and prices in real time to the brokerage and investment community. The industry focused on purchasers—IT managers—who valued standardized systems, which made their lives easier. This made no sense to Bloomberg. Traders and analysts, not IT managers, make or lose millions of dollars for their employers each day. Profit opportunities come from disparities in information. When markets are active, traders and analysts must make rapid decisions. Every second counts. So Bloomberg designed a system specifically to offer traders better value, one with easy-to-use terminals and keyboards labeled with familiar financial terms. The systems also have two flat-panel monitors so that traders can see all the information they need at once without having to open and close numerous windows. Because traders must analyze information before they act, Bloomberg added a built-in analytic capability that works with the press of a button. Before, traders and analysts had to download data and use a pencil and calculators to perform important financial calculations. Now users can quickly run "what if" scenarios to compute returns on alternative investments, and they can perform longitudinal analyses of historical data. By focusing on users, Bloomberg was also able to see the paradox of traders' and analysts' personal lives. They have tremendous income but work such long hours that they have little time to spend it. Realizing that markets have slow times during the day when little trading takes place, Bloomberg decided to add information and purchasing services aimed at enhancing traders' personal lives. Traders can use these services to buy items such as flowers, clothing, and jewelry; make travel arrangements; get information about wines; or search through real estate listings. By shifting its focus upstream from purchasers to users, Bloomberg created a value curve that was radically different from anything the industry had seen before. The traders and analysts wielded their power within their firms to force IT managers to purchase Bloomberg terminals. Many industries afford similar opportunities to create blue oceans. By questioning conventional definitions of who can and should be the target buyer, companies can often see fundamentally new ways to unlock value. Consider how Canon copiers created the small desktop copier industry by shifting the target customer of the copier industry from corporate purchasers to users. Or how SAP shifted the customer focus of the business application software industry from the functional user to the corporate purchaser to create its enormously successful real-time integrated software business. What is the chain of buyers in your industry? Which buyer group does your industry typically focus on? If you shifted the buyer group of your industry, how could you unlock new value? Path 4: Look Across Complementary Product and Service Offerings Few products and services are used in a vacuum. In most cases, other products and services affect their value. But in most industries, rivals converge within the bounds of their industry's product and service offerings. Take movie theaters. The ease and cost of getting a babysitter and parking the car affect the perceived value of going to the movies. Yet these complementary services are beyond the bounds of the movie theater industry as it has been traditionally defined. Few cinema operators worry about how hard or costly it is for people to get babysitters. But they should, because it affects demand for their business. Imagine a movie theater with a babysitting service. Untapped value is often hidden in complementary products and services. The key is to define the total solution buyers seek when they choose a product or service. A simple way to do so is to think about what happens before, during, and after your product is used. Babysitting and parking the car are needed before people can go to the movies. Operating and application software are used along with computer hardware. In the airline industry, ground transportation is used after the flight but is clearly part of what the customer needs to travel from one place to another. Consider NABI, a Hungarian bus company. It applied path 4 to the $1 billion U.S. transit bus industry. The major customers in the industry are public transport properties (PTPs), municipally

owned transportation companies serving fixed-route public bus transportation in major cities or counties. Under the accepted rules of competition in the industry, companies competed to offer the lowest purchase price. Designs were outdated, delivery times were late, quality was low, and the price of options was prohibitive given the industry's penny-pinching approach. To NABI, however, none of this made sense. Why were bus companies focused only on the initial purchase price of the bus, when municipalities kept buses in circulation for twelve years on average? When it framed the market in this way, NABI saw insights that had escaped the entire industry. NABI discovered that the highest-cost element to municipalities was not the price of the bus per se, the factor the whole industry competed on, but rather the costs that came after the bus was purchased: the maintenance of running the bus over its twelve-year life cycle. Repairs after traffic accidents, fuel usage, wear and tear on parts that frequently needed to be replaced due to the bus's heavy weight, preventive body work to stop rusting, and the like— these were the highest-cost factors to municipalities. With new demands for clean air being placed on municipalities, the cost for public transport not being environmentally friendly was also beginning to be felt. Yet despite all these costs, which outstripped the initial bus price, the industry had virtually overlooked the complementary activity of maintenance and life-cycle costs. This made NABI realize that the transit bus industry did not have to be a commodity-price-driven industry but that bus companies, focusing on selling buses at the lowest possible price, had made it that way. By looking at the total solution of complementary activities, NABI created a bus unlike any the industry had seen before. Buses were normally made from steel, which was heavy, corrosive, and hard to repair after accidents because entire panels had to be replaced. NABI adopted fiberglass in making its buses, a practice that killed five birds with one stone. Fiberglass bodies substantially cut the costs of preventive maintenance by being corrosion-free. It made body repairs faster, cheaper, and easier because fiberglass does not require panel replacements for dents and accidents; rather, damaged parts are simply cut out and new fiberglass materials are easily soldered. At the same time, its light weight (30–35 percent lighter than steel) cut fuel consumption and emissions substantially, making the buses more environmentally friendly. Moreover, its light weight allowed NABI to use not only lower-powered engines but also fewer axles, resulting in lower manufacturing costs and more space inside the bus. In this way, NABI created a value curve that is radically divergent from the industry's average curve. As you can see in figure 3-3, by building its buses in lightweight fiberglass, NABI eliminated or significantly reduced costs related to corrosion prevention, maintenance, and fuel consumption. As a result, even though NABI charged a higher initial purchase price than the average price of the industry, it offered its buses at a much lower life-cycle cost to municipalities. With much lighter emissions, the NABI buses.

the level of environmental friendliness high above the industry standard. Moreover, the higher price NABI charged allowed it to create factors unprecedented in the industry, such as modern aesthetic design and customer friendliness, including lower floors for easy mounting and more seats for less standing. These boosted demand for transit bus service, generating more revenues for municipalities. NABI changed the way municipalities saw their revenues and costs involved in transit bus service. NABI created exceptional value for the buyers—in this case for both municipalities and end users—at a low life-cycle cost. Not surprisingly, both municipalities and riders loved the new buses. NABI has captured 20 percent of the U.S. market since its inception in 1993, quickly vying for the number one slot in market share, growth, and profitability. NABI, based in Hungary, created a blue ocean that made the competition irrelevant in the United States, creating a win-win for all: itself, municipalities, and citizens. It has accumulated more than $1 billion in orders and was named by the Economist Intelligence Unit in October 2002 as one of the thirty most successful companies in the world. Similarly, consider the British teakettle industry, which, despite its importance to British culture, had flat sales and shrinking profit margins until Philips Electronics came along with a teakettle that turned the red ocean blue. By thinking in terms of complementary products and services, Philips saw that the biggest issue the British had in brewing tea was not in the kettle itself but in the complementary product of water, which had to be boiled in the kettle. The issue was the lime scale found in tap water. The lime scale accumulated in kettles as the water was boiled, and later found its way into the freshly brewed tea. The phlegmatic British typically took a teaspoon and went fishing to capture the off-putting lime scale before drinking home-brewed tea. To the kettle industry, the water issue was not its problem. It was the problem of another industry—the public water supply. By thinking in terms of solving the major pain points in customers' total solution, Philips saw the water problem as its opportunity. The result: Philips created a kettle having a mouth filter that effectively captured the lime scale as the water was poured. Lime scale would never again be found swimming in British homebrewed tea. The industry was again kick-started on a strong growth trajectory as people began replacing their old kettles with the new filtered kettles. There are many other examples of companies that have followed this path to create a blue ocean. Borders and Barnes & Noble (B&N) superstores redefined the scope of the services they offer. They transformed the product they sell from the book itself into the pleasure of reading and intellectual exploration, adding lounges, knowledgeable staff, and coffee bars to create an environment that celebrates reading and learning. In less than six years, Borders and B&N emerged as the two largest bookstore chains in the United States, with more than one thousand seventy superstores between them. Virgin Entertainment's megastores combine CDs, videos, computer games, and stereo and audio equipment to satisfy buyers' complete entertainment needs. Dyson designs its vacuum cleaners to eliminate the cost and annoyance of having to buy and change vacuum cleaner bags. Zeneca's Salick cancer centers combine all the cancer treatments their patients might need under one roof so that they don't have to go from one specialized center to another, making separate appointments for each service they require. What is the context in which your product or service is used? What happens before, during, and after? Can you identify the pain points? How can you eliminate these pain points through a complementary product or service offering? Path 5: Look Across Functional or Emotional Appeal to Buyers Competition in an industry tends to converge not only on an accepted notion of the scope of its products and services but also on one of two possible bases of appeal. Some industries competeprincipally on price and function largely on calculations of utility; their appeal is rational. Other industries compete largely on feelings; their appeal is emotional. Yet the appeal of most products or services is rarely intrinsically one or the other. Rather it is usually a result of the way companies have competed in the past, which has unconsciously educated consumers on what to expect. Companies' behavior affects buyers' expectations in a reinforcing cycle. Over time, functionally oriented industries become more functionally oriented; emotionally oriented industries become more emotionally oriented. No wonder market research rarely reveals new insights into what attracts customers. Industries have trained customers in what to expect. When surveyed, they echo back: more of the same for less. When companies are willing to challenge the functionalemotional orientation of their industry, they often find new market space. We have observed two common patterns. Emotionally oriented industries offer many extras that add price without enhancing functionality. Stripping away those extras may create a fundamentally simpler, lower-priced, lower-cost business model that customers would welcome. Conversely, functionally oriented industries can often infuse commodity products with new life by adding a dose of emotion and, in so doing, can stimulate new demand. Two well-known examples are Swatch, which transformed the functionally driven budget watch industry into an emotionally driven fashion statement, or The Body Shop, which did the reverse, transforming the emotionally driven industry of cosmetics into a functional, no-nonsense cosmetics house. In addition, consider the experience of QB (Quick Beauty) House. QB House created a blue ocean in the Japanese barbershop industry and is rapidly growing throughout Asia. Started in 1996 in Tokyo, QB House has blossomed from one outlet in 1996 to more than two hundred shops in 2003. The number of visitors surged from 57,000 in 1996 to 3.5 million annually in 2002. The company is expanding in Singapore and Malaysia and is targeting one thousand outlets in Asia by 2013. At the heart of QB House's blue ocean strategy is a shift in the Asian barbershop industry from an emotional industry to a highly.

functional one. In Japan the time it takes to get a man's haircut hovers around one hour. Why? A long process of activities is undertaken to make the haircutting experience a ritual. Numerous hot towels are applied, shoulders are rubbed and massaged, customers are served tea and coffee, and the barber follows a ritual in cutting hair, including special hair and skin treatments such as blow drying and shaving. The result is that the actual time spent cutting hair is a fraction of the total time. Moreover, these actions create a long queue for other potential customers. The price of this haircutting process is 3,000 to 5,000 yen ($27 to $45). QB House changed all that. It recognized that many people, especially working professionals, do not wish to waste an hour on a haircut. So QB House stripped away the emotional service elements of hot towels, shoulder rubs, and tea and coffee. It also dramatically reduced special hair treatments and focused mainly on basic cuts. QB House then went one step further, eliminating the traditional time-consuming wash-and-dry practice by creating the "air wash" system—an overhead hose that is pulled down to "vacuum" every cut-off hair. This new system works much better and faster, without getting the customer's head wet. These changes reduced the haircutting time from one hour to ten minutes. Moreover, outside each shop is a traffic light system that indicates when a haircut slot is available. This removes waiting time uncertainty and eliminates the reservation desk. In this way, QB House was able to reduce the price of a haircut to 1,000 yen ($9) versus the industry average of 3,000 to 5,000 yen ($27–$45) while raising the hourly revenue earned per barber nearly 50 percent, with lower staff costs and less required retail space per barber. QB House created this "no-nonsense" haircutting service with improved hygiene. It introduced not only a sanitation facility set up for each chair but also a "one-use" policy, where every customer is provided with a new set of towel and comb. To appreciate its blue ocean creation, see figure 3-4. Cemex, the world's third-largest cement producer, is another company that created a blue ocean by shifting the orientation of its industry—this time in the reverse direction, from functional toemotional. In Mexico, cement sold in retail bags to the average doit-yourselfer represents more than 85 percent of the total cement market.4 As it stood, however, the market was unattractive. There were far more noncustomers than customers. Even though most poor families owned their own land and cement was sold as a relatively inexpensive functional input material, the Mexican population lived in chronic overcrowding. Few families built additions, and those that did took on average four to seven years to build only one additional room. Why? Most of the families' extra money was spent on village festivals, quinceañeras (girls' fifteen-year birthday parties), baptisms, and weddings. Contributing to these important milestone events was a chance to distinguish oneself in the community, whereas not contributing would be a sign of arrogance and disrespect. As a result, most of Mexico's poor had insufficient and inconsistent savings to purchase building materials, even though having acement house was the stuff of dreams in Mexico. Cemex conservatively estimated that this market could grow to be worth $500 million to $600 million annually if it could unlock this latent demand.5 Cemex's answer to this dilemma came in 1998 with its launch of the Patrimonio Hoy program, which shifted the orientation of cement from a functional product to the gift of dreams. When people bought cement they were on the path to building rooms of love, where laughter and happiness could be shared—what better gift could there be? At the foundation of Patrimonio Hoy was the traditional Mexican system of tandas, a traditional community savings scheme. In a tanda, ten individuals (for example) contribute 100 pesos per week for ten weeks. In the first week, lots are drawn to see who "wins" the 1,000 pesos ($93) in each of the ten weeks. All participants win the 1,000 pesos one time only, but when they win, they receive a large amount to make a large purchase. In traditional tandas the "winning" family would spend the windfall on an important festive or religious event such as a baptism or marriage. In the Patrimonio Hoy, however, the supertanda is directed toward building room additions with cement. Think of it as a form of wedding registry, except that instead of giving, for example, silverware, Cemex positioned cement as a loving gift. The Patrimonio Hoy building materials club that Cemex set up consisted of a group of roughly seventy people contributing on average 120 pesos each week for seventy weeks. The winner of the supertanda each week, however, did not receive the total sum in pesos but rather received the equivalent building materials to complete an entire new room. Cemex complemented the winnings with the delivery of the cement to the winner's home, construction classes on how to effectively build rooms, and a technical adviser who maintained a relationship with the participants during their project. Whereas Cemex's competitors sold bags of cement,

Cemex was selling a dream, with a business model involving innovative financing and construction know-how. Cemex went a step further, throwing small festivities for the town when a room was finished and thereby reinforcing the happiness it brought to people and the tanda tradition. Since the company launched this new emotional orientation of Cemex cement coupled with its funding and technical services, demand for cement has soared. Around 20 percent more families are building additional rooms, and families are planning to build two to three more rooms than originally planned. In a market that competed on price with slow growth, Cemex enjoys 15 percent monthly growth, selling its cement at higher prices (roughly 3.5 pesos). Cemex has so far tripled cement consumption by the mass of do-it-yourself homebuilders—from 2,300 pounds consumed every four years, on average, to the same amount being consumed in fifteen months. The predictability of the quantities of cement sold through the supertandas also drops Cemex's cost structure via lower inventory costs, smoother production runs, and guaranteed sales that lower costs of capital. Social pressure makes defaults on supertanda payments rare. Overall, Cemex created a blue ocean of emotional cement that achieved differentiation at a low cost. Similarly, with its wildly successful Viagra, Pfizer shifted the focus from medical treatment to lifestyle enhancement. Likewise, consider how Starbucks turned the coffee industry on its head by shifting its focus from commodity coffee sales to the emotional atmosphere in which customers enjoy their coffee. A burst of blue ocean creation is under way in a number of service industries but in the opposite direction—moving from an emotional to a functional orientation. Relationship businesses, such as insurance, banking, and investing, have relied heavily on the emotional bond between broker and client. They are ripe for change. Direct Line Group, a U.K. insurance company, for example, has done away with traditional brokers. It reasoned that customers would not need the hand-holding and emotional comfort that brokers traditionally provide if the company did a better job of, for example, paying claims rapidly and eliminating complicated paperwork. So instead of using brokers and regional branch offices, Direct Line uses information technology to improve claims handling, and it

passes on some of the cost savings to customers in the form of lower insurance premiums. In the United States, The Vanguard Group (in index funds) and Charles Schwab (in brokerage services) are doing the same thing in the investment industry, creating a blue ocean by transforming emotionally oriented businesses based on personal relationships into high-performance, low-cost functional businesses. Does your industry compete on functionality or emotional appeal? If you compete on emotional appeal, what elements can you strip out to make it functional? If you compete on functionality, what elements can be added to make it emotional? Path 6: Look Across Time All industries are subject to external trends that affect their businesses over time. Think of the rapid rise of the Internet or the global movement toward protecting the environment. Looking at these trends with the right perspective can show you how to create blue ocean opportunities. Most companies adapt incrementally and somewhat passively as events unfold. Whether it's the emergence of new technologies or major regulatory changes, managers tend to focus on projecting the trend itself. That is, they ask in which direction a technology will evolve, how it will be adopted, whether it will become scalable. They pace their own actions to keep up with the development of the trends they're tracking. But key insights into blue ocean strategy rarely come from projecting the trend itself. Instead they arise from business insights into how the trend will change value to customers and impact the company's business model. By looking across time—from the value a market delivers today to the value it might deliver tomorrow— managers can actively shape their future and lay claim to a new blue ocean. Looking across time is perhaps more difficult than the previous approaches we've discussed, but it can be made subject to the same disciplined approach. We're not talking about predicting the future, something that is inherently impossible. Rather, we're talking about finding insight in trends that are observable today. Three principles are critical to assessing trends across time. To form the basis of a blue ocean strategy, these trends must be decisive to your business, they must be irreversible, and they must have a clear trajectory. Many trends can be observed at any one time— for example, a discontinuity in technology, the rise of a new lifestyle, or a change in regulatory or social environments. But usually only one or two will have a decisive impact on any particular business. And it may be possible to see a trend or major event without being able to predict its direction. In 1998, for example, the mounting Asian crisis was an important trend certain to have a big impact on financial services. But it was impossible to predict the direction that trend would take, and therefore it would have been a risky enterprise to envision a blue ocean strategy that might result from it. In contrast, the euro has been evolving along a constant trajectory as it has been replacing Europe's multiple currencies. It is a decisive, irreversible, and clearly developing trend in financial services upon which blue oceans can be created as the European Union continues to enlarge. Having identified a trend of this nature, you can then look across time and ask yourself what the market would look like if the trend were taken to its logical conclusion. Working back from that vision of a blue ocean strategy, you can identify what must be changed today to unlock a new blue ocean. For example, Apple observed the flood of illegal music file sharing that began in the late 1990s. Music file sharing programs such as Napster, Kazaa, and LimeWire had created a network of Internetsavvy music lovers freely, yet illegally, sharing music across the globe. By 2003 more than two billion illegal music files were being traded every month. While the recording industry fought to stop the cannibalization of physical CDs, illegal digital music downloading continued to grow. With the technology out there for anyone to digitally download music free instead of paying $19 for an average CD, the trend toward digital music was clear. This trend was underscored by the fastgrowing demand for MP3 players that played mobile digital music, such as Apple's hit iPod. Apple capitalized on this decisive trend with a clear trajectory by launching the iTunes online music store in 2003. In agreement with five major music companies—BMG, EMI Group, Sony, Universal Music Group, and Warner Brothers Records—iTunes offered legal, easy-to-use, and flexible à la carte song downloads. iTunes allowed buyers to freely browse two hundred thousand songs, listen to thirty-second samples, and download an individual song for 99 cents or an entire album for $9.99. By allowing people to buy individual songs and strategically pricing them far more reasonably, iTunes broke a key customer annoyance factor: the need to purchase an entire CD when they wanted only one or two songs on it. iTunes also leapt past free downloading services, providing sound quality as well as intuitive navigating, searching, and browsing functions. To illegally download music you must first search for the song, album, or artist. If you are looking for a complete album you must know the names of all the songs and their order. It is rare to find a complete album to download in one location. The sound quality is consistently poor because most people burn CDs at a low bit rate to save space. And most of the tracks available reflect the tastes of sixteen-year-olds, so although theoretically there are billions of tracks available, the scope is limited. In contrast, Apple's search and browsing functions are considered the best in the business. Moreover, iTunes music editors include a number of added features usually found in the record shops, including iTunes essentials such as Best Hair Bands or Best Love Songs, staff favorites, celebrity play lists, and Billboard charts. And the iTunes sound quality is the highest because iTunes encodes songs in a format called AAC, which offers sound quality superior to MP3s, even those burned at a very high data rate. Customers have been flocking to iTunes, and recording companies and artists are also winning. Under iTunes they receive 65 percent of the purchase price of digitally downloaded songs, at last .

financially benefiting from the digital downloading craze. In addition, Apple further protected recording companies by devising copyright protection that would not inconvenience users—who had grown accustomed to the freedom of digital music in the postNapster world—but would satisfy the music industry. The iTunes Music Store allows users to burn songs onto iPods and CDs up to seven times, enough to easily satisfy music lovers but far too few times to make professional piracy an issue. Today the iTunes Music Store offers more than 700,000 songs and has sold more than 70 million songs in its first year, with users downloading on average 2.5 million per week. Nielsen//NetRatings estimates that the iTunes Music Store now accounts for 70 percent of the legal music download market. Apple's iTunes is unlocking a blue ocean in digital music, with the added advantage of increasing the attractiveness of its already hot iPod player. As other online music stores enter the fray, the challenge for Apple will be to keep its sights on the evolving mass market and not to fall into competitive benchmarking or high-end niche marketing. Similarly, Cisco Systems created a new market space by thinking across time trends. It started with a decisive and irreversible trend that had a clear trajectory: the growing demand for high-speed data exchange. Cisco looked at the world as it was and concluded that the world was hampered by slow data rates and incompatible computer networks. Demand was exploding as, among other factors, the number of Internet users doubled roughly every one hundred days. So Cisco could clearly see that the problem would inevitably worsen. Cisco's routers, switches, and other networking devices were designed to create breakthrough value for customers, offering fast data exchanges in a seamless networking environment. Thus Cisco's insight is as much about value innovation as it is about technology. Today more than 80 percent of all traffic on the Internet goes through Cisco's products, and its gross margins in this new market space have been in the 60 percent range. Similarly, a host of other companies are creating blue oceans by applying path 6. Consider how CNN created the first real-time twenty-four-hour global news network based on the rising tide of globalization. Or how HBO's hit show Sex and the City acted on the trend of increasingly urban and successful women who struggle to find love and marry later in life. What trends have a high probability of impacting your industry, are irreversible, and are evolving in a clear trajectory? How will these trends impact your industry? Given this, how can you open up unprecedented customer utility? Conceiving New Market Space By thinking across conventional boundaries of competition, you can see how to make convention-altering, strategic moves that reconstruct established market boundaries and create blue oceans. The process of discovering and creating blue oceans is not about predicting or preempting industry trends. Nor is it a trial-and-error process of implementing wild new business ideas that happen to come across managers' minds or intuition. Rather, managers are engaged in a structured process of reordering market realities in a fundamentally new way. Through reconstructing existing market elements across industry and market boundaries, they will be able to free themselves from head-to-head competition in the red ocean. Figure 3-5 summarizes the six-path framework. We are now ready to move on to building your strategy planning process around these six paths. We next look at how you reframe your strategy planning process to focus on the big picture and apply these ideas in formulating your own blue ocean strategy.

CHAPTER SEVEN

Focus on the Big Picture, Not the Numbers

Y OU NOW KNOW THE PATHS to creating blue oceans. The next question is, How do you align your strategic planning process to focus on the big picture and apply these ideas in drawing your company's strategy canvas to arrive at a blue ocean strategy? This is no small challenge. Our research reveals that most companies' strategic planning process keeps them wedded to red oceans. The process tends to drive companies to compete within existing market space. Think of a typical strategic plan. It starts with a lengthy description of current industry conditions and the competitive situation. Next is a discussion of how to increase market share, capture new segments, or cut costs, followed by an outline of numerous goals and initiatives. A full budget is almost invariably attached, as are lavish graphs and a surfeit of spreadsheets. The process usually culminates in the preparation of a large document culled from a mishmash of data provided by people from various parts of the organization who often have conflicting agendas and poor communication. In this process, managers spend the majority of strategic thinking time filling in boxes and running numbers instead of thinking outside the box and developing a clear picture of how to break from the competition. If you ask companies to present their proposed strategies in no more than a few slides, it is not surprising that few clear or compelling strategies are articulated. It's no wonder that few strategic plans lead to the creation of blue oceans or are translated into action. Executives are paralyzed by the muddle. Few employees deep down in the company even know what the strategy is. And a closer look reveals that most plans don't contain a strategy at all but rather a smorgasbord of tactics that individually make sense but collectively don't add up to a unified, clear direction that sets a company apart—let alone makes the competition irrelevant. Does this sound like the strategic plans in your company? This brings us to the second principle of blue ocean strategy: Focus on the big picture, not the numbers. This principle is key to mitigating the planning risk of investing lots of effort and lots of time but delivering only tactical red ocean moves. Here we develop an alternative approach to the existing strategic planning process that is based not on preparing a document but on drawing a strategy canvas.1 This approach consistently produces strategies that unlock the creativity of a wide range of people within an organization, open companies' eyes to blue oceans, and are easy to understand and communicate for effective execution. Focusing on the Big Picture In our research and consulting work, we have found that drawing a strategy canvas not only visualizes a company's current strategic position in its marketplace but also helps it chart its future strategy. By building a company's strategic planning process around a strategy canvas, a company and its managers focus their main attention on the big picture rather than becoming immersed in numbers and jargon and getting caught up in operational details.

As previous chapters reveal, drawing a strategy canvas does three things. First, it shows the strategic profile of an industry by depicting very clearly the factors (and the possible future factors) that affect competition among industry players. Second, it shows the strategic profile of current and potential competitors, identifying which factors they invest in strategically. Finally, it shows the company's strategic profile—or value curve—depicting how it invests in the factors of competition and how it might invest in them in the future. As discussed in chapter 2, the strategic profile with high blue ocean potential has three complementary qualities: focus, divergence, and a compelling tagline. If a company's strategic profile does not clearly reveal those qualities, its strategy will likely be muddled, undifferentiated, and hard to communicate. It is also likely to be costly to execute. Drawing Your Strategy Canvas Drawing a strategy canvas is never easy. Even identifying the key factors of competition is far from straightforward. As you will see, the final list is usually very different from the first draft. Assessing to what extent your company and its competitors offer the various competitive factors is equally challenging. Most managers have a strong impression of how they and their competitors fare along one or two dimensions within their own scope of responsibility, but very few can see the overall dynamics of their industry. The catering manager of an airline, for example, will be highly sensitive to how the airline compares in terms of refreshments.

But that focus makes consistent measurement difficult; what seems to be a very big difference to the catering manager may not be important to customers, who look at the complete offering. Some managers will define the competitive factors according to internal benefits. For example, a CIO might prize the company's IT infrastructure for its data-mining capacity, a feature lost on most customers, who are more concerned with speed and ease of use.

Over the past ten years, we have developed a structured process for drawing and discussing a strategy canvas that pushes a company's strategy toward a blue ocean. A 150-year-old financial services group that we'll call European Financial Services (EFS) is one of the companies that adopted this process to develop a strategy that breaks away from the competition. The resulting EFS strategy yielded a 30 percent revenue boost in its initial year. The process, which builds on the six paths of creating blue oceans and involves a lot of visual stimulation in order to unlock people's creativity, has four major steps.

Step 1: Visual Awakening A common mistake is to discuss changes in strategy before resolving differences of opinion about the current state of play. Another problem is that executives are often reluctant to accept the need for change; they may have a vested interest in the status quo, or they may feel that time will eventually vindicate their previous choices.

Indeed, when we ask executives what prompts them to seek out blue oceans and introduce change, they usually say that it takes a highly determined leader or a serious crisis. Fortunately, we've found that asking executives to draw the value curve of their company's strategy brings home the need for change. It serves as a forceful wake-up call for companies to challenge their existing strategies. That was the experience at EFS, which had been struggling for a long time with an ill-defined and poorly communicated strategy. The company was also deeply divided. The top executives of EFS's regional subsidiaries bitterly resented what they saw as the arrogance of the corporate executives, whose philosophy, they believed, was essentially "nuts in the field, brains in the center." That conflict made it all the more difficult for EFS to come to grips with its strategic problems. Yet before the firm could chart a new strategy, it was essential that it reach a common understanding of its current position. EFS began the strategy process by bringing together more than twenty senior managers from subsidiaries in Europe, North America, Asia, and Australia and splitting them into two teams. One team was responsible for producing a value curve depicting EFS's current strategic profile in its traditional corporate foreign exchange business relative to its competitors. The other team was charged with the same task for EFS's emerging online foreign exchange business. They were given ninety minutes, because if EFS had a clear strategy, surely it would emerge quickly. It was a painful experience. Both teams had heated debates about what constituted a competitive factor and what the factors were. Different factors were important, it seemed, in different regions and even for different customer segments. For example, Europeans argued that in its traditional business, EFS had to offer consulting services on risk management, given the perceived riskaverse nature of its customers. Americans, however, dismissed that as largely irrelevant. They stressed the value of speed and ease of use. Many people had pet ideas of which they were the sole champions. One person in the online team argued, for example, that customerswould be drawn in by the promise of instant confirmations of their transactions—a service no one else thought necessary. Despite these difficulties, the teams completed their assignments and presented their pictures in a general meeting of all participants. The pictures clearly revealed defects in the company's strategy. EFS's traditional and online value curves both demonstrated a serious lack of focus; the company was investing in diverse and numerous factors in both businesses. What's more, EFS's two curves were very similar to those of competitors. Not surprisingly, neither team could come up with a memorable tagline that was true to the team's value curve. The pictures also highlighted contradictions. The online business, for example, had invested heavily in making the Web site easy to use—it had even won awards for this—but it became apparent.that speed had been overlooked. EFS had one of the slowest Web sites in the business, and that might explain why such a wellregarded site did a relatively poor job of attracting customers and converting them into sales. The sharpest shocks, perhaps, came from comparing EFS's strategy with its competitors'. The online group realized that its strongest competitor, which we've called Clearskies, had a focused, original, and easily communicable strategy: "One-click E-Z FX." Clearskies, which was growing rapidly, was swimming away from the red ocean. Faced with direct evidence of the company's shortcomings, EFS's executives could not defend what they had shown to be a weak, unoriginal, and poorly communicated strategy. Trying to draw the strategy canvases had made a stronger case for change than any argument based on numbers and words could have done. This created a strong desire in top management to seriously rethink the company's current strategy.

Step 2: Visual Exploration Getting the wake-up call is only the first step. The next step is to send a team into the field, putting managers face-to-face with what they must make sense of: how people use or don't use their products or services. This step may seem obvious, but we have found that managers often outsource this part of the strategy-making process. They rely on reports that other people (often at one or two removes from the world they report on) have put together. A company should never outsource its eyes. There is simply no substitute for seeing for yourself. Great artists don't paint from other people's descriptions or even from photographs; they like to see the subject for themselves. The same is true for great strategists. Michael Bloomberg, before becoming mayor of New York City, was hailed as a business visionary for his realization that the providers of financial information also needed to provide online analytics to help users make sense of the data. But he would be the first to tell you that the idea should have been obvious to anyone who had ever watched traders using Reuters or Dow Jones Telerate. Before Bloomberg, traders used paper, pencil, and handheld calculators to write down price quotes and figure fair market values before making buy and sell decisions, a practice that cost them time and money as well as built-in errors. Great strategic insights like this are less the product of genius than of getting into the field and challenging the boundaries of competition.3 In the case of Bloomberg, his insight came by switching the focus of the industry from IT purchasers to users: the traders and analysts. This allowed him to see what was invisible to others.4 Obviously, the first port of call should be the customers. But you should not stop there. You should also go after noncustomers.5 And when the customer is not the same as the user, you need to extend your observations to the users, as Bloomberg did. You should not only talk to these people but also watch them in action. Identifying the array of complementary products and services that are consumed alongside your own may give you insight into bundling opportunities. For example, parents who go to the movies will engage a babysitter for the night. As the European cinema operator Kinepolis discovered, adding on-site childcare services helped fill European cinemas. Finally, you need to look at how customers might find alternative ways of fulfilling the need that your product or service satisfies. For example, driving is an alternative to flying, so you should also examine its distinct advantages and characteristics. EFS sent its managers into the field for four weeks to explore the six paths to creating blue oceans.6 In this process, each was to interview and observe ten people involved in corporate foreign exchange, including lost customers, new customers, and the customers of EFS's competitors and alternatives. The managers also reached outside the industry's traditional boundaries to companies that did not yet use corporate foreign exchange services but that might in the future, such as Internet-based companies with a global reach like Amazon.com. They interviewed the end users of corporate foreign exchange services—the accounting and treasury departments of companies. And finally, they looked at ancillary products and services that their customers used—in particular, treasury management and pricing simulations. The field research overturned many of the conclusions managers had reached in the first step of the strategy creation process. For example, account relationship managers, whom nearly everyone had agreed were a key to success and on whom EFS prided itself, turned out to be the company's Achilles' heel. Customers hated wasting time dealing with relationship managers. To buyers, relationship managers were seen as relationship savers because EFS failed to deliver on its promises. To everyone's astonishment, the factor customers valued most was getting speedy confirmation of transactions, which only one manager had previously suggested was important. The EFS managers saw that their customers' accounting department personnel spent a lot of time making phone calls to confirm that payments had been made and to check when they would be received. Customers received numerous calls on the same subject, and the time wasted in handling them was compounded by the necessity of making further calls to the foreign exchange provider, namely EFS or a competitor. EFS's teams were then sent back to the drawing board. This time, though, they had to propose a new strategy. Each team had to draw six new value curves using the six path framework explained in chapter 3. Each new value curve had to depict a strategy that would make the company stand out in its market. By demanding six pictures from each team, we hoped to push managers to create innovative proposals and break the boundaries of their conventional thinking. For each visual strategy, the teams also had to write a compelling tagline that captured the essence of the strategy and spoke directly to buyers. Suggestions included "Leave It to Us," "Make Me Smarter," and "Transactions in Trust." A strong sense of competition developed between the two teams, making the process fun, imbuing it with energy, and driving the teams to develop blue ocean strategies. Step 3: Visual Strategy Fair After two weeks of drawing and redrawing, the teams presented their strategy canvases at what we call a visual strategy fair. Attendees included senior corporate executives but consisted mainly of representatives of EFS's external constituencies—the kinds of people the managers had met with during their field trips, including noncustomers, customers of competitors, and some of the most demanding EFS customers. In two hours, the teams presented all twelve curves—six by the online group, and six by the offline group. They were given no more than ten minutes to present each curve, on the theory that any idea that takes more than ten minutes to communicate is probably too complicated to be any good. The pictures were hung on the walls so that the audience could easily see them. After the twelve strategies were presented, each judge—an invited attendee—was given five sticky notes and told to put them next to his or her favorites. The judges could put all five on a single strategy if they found it that compelling. The transparency and immediacy of this approach freed it from the politics that sometimes seem endemic to the strategic planning process. Managers had to rely on the originality and clarity of their curves and their pitches. One began, for example, with the line, "We've got a strategy so cunning that you won't be our customers, you'll be our fans." After the notes were posted, the judges were asked to explain their picks, adding another level of feedback to the strategy-making process. Judges were also asked to explain why they did not vote for the other value curves. As the teams synthesized the judges' common likes and dislikes, they realized that fully one-third of what they had thought were key competitive factors were, in fact, marginal to customers. Another one-third either were not well articulated or had been overlooked in the visual awakening phase. It was clear that the executives needed to reassess some long-held assumptions, such as EFS's separation of its online and traditional businesses. They also learned that buyers from all markets had a basic set of needs and expected similar services. If you met those common needs, customers would happily forgo everything else. Regional differences became significant only when there was a problem with the basics. This was news to many people who had claimed that their regions were unique. Following the strategy fair, the teams were finally able to complete their mission. They were able to draw a value curve that was a truer likeness of the existing strategic profile than anything they had produced earlier, in part because the new picture ignored the specious distinction that EFS had made between its online and offline businesses. More important, the managers were now in a position to draw a future strategy that would be distinctive as well as speak to a true but hidden need in the marketplace. Figure 4-4 highlights the stark differences between the company's current and future strategies. As the figure shows, EFS's future strategy eliminated relationship management and reduced investment in account executives, who, from this point on, were assigned only to "AAA" accounts. These moves dramatically reduced EFS's costs because relationship managers and account executives were the highest-cost element of its business. EFS's future strategy emphasized ease of use, security, accuracy, and speed. These factors would be delivered through computerization, which would allow customers to input data directly instead of having to send a fax to EFS. This action would also free up corporate dealers' time, a large portion of which had been spent completing paperwork and correcting errors. Dealers would now be able to provide richer market commentary, a key success factor. Using the Internet, EFS would send automatic confirmations to all customers. And it would offer a payment-tracking service, just as FedEx and UPS do for parcels. The foreign exchange industry had never offered these services before. summarizes EFS's four actions to create value innovation, the cornerstone of blue ocean strategy.

The new value curve exhibited the criteria of a successful strategy. It displayed more focus than the previous strategy; investments that were made were given a much stronger commitment than before. It also stood apart from the industry's existing me-too curves and lent itself to a compelling tagline: "The FedEx of corporate foreign exchange: easy, reliable, fast, and trackable." By collapsing its online and traditional businesses into one compelling offering, EFS substantially cut the operational complexity of its business model, making systematic execution far easier. Step 4: Visual Communication After the future strategy is set, the last step is to communicate it in a way that can be easily understood by any employee. EFS distributed the one-page picture showing its new and old strategic profiles so that every employee could see where the company stood and where it had to focus its efforts to create a compelling future. The senior managers who participated in developing the strategy held The new value curve exhibited the criteria of a successful strategy. It displayed more focus than the previous strategy; investments that were made were given a much stronger commitment than before. It also stood apart from the industry's existing me-too curves and lent itself to a compelling tagline: "The FedEx of corporate foreign exchange: easy, reliable, fast, and trackable." By collapsing its online and traditional businesses into one compelling offering, EFS substantially cut the operational complexity of its business model, making systematic execution far easier. Step 4: Visual Communication After the future strategy is set, the last step is to communicate it in a way that can be easily understood by any employee. EFS distributed the one-page picture showing its new and old strategic profiles so that every employee could see where the company stood and where it had to focus its efforts to create a compelling future. The senior managers who participated in developing the strategy held meetings with their direct reports to walk them through the picture, explaining what needed to be eliminated, reduced, raised, and created to pursue a blue ocean. Those people passed the message on to their direct reports. Employees were so motivated by the clear game plan that many pinned up a version of the picture in their cubicles as a reminder of EFS's new priorities and the gaps that needed to be closed. The new picture became a reference point for all investment decisions. Only those ideas that would help EFS move from the old to the new value curve were given the go-ahead. When, for example, regional offices requested that the IT department add links on the Web site—something that in the past would have been agreed to without debate—IT asked them to explain how the new links helped move EFS toward its new profile. If the regional offices couldn't provide an explanation, the request was denied, thereby promoting clarity and not confusion on the Web site. Similarly, when the IT department pitched a multimillion-dollar back-office system to top management, the system's ability to meet the new value curve's strategic needs was the chief metric by which it was judged. Visualizing Strategy at the Corporate Level Visualizing strategy can also greatly inform the dialogue among individual business units and the corporate center in transforming a company from a red ocean to a blue ocean player. When business units present their strategy canvases to one another, they deepen their understanding of the other businesses in the corporate portfolio. Moreover, the process also fosters the transfer of strategic best practices across units. Using the Strategy Canvas To see how this works, consider how Samsung Electronics of Korea used strategy canvases at its 2000 corporate conference, which was attended by more than seventy top managers, including the CEO. Unit heads presented their canvases and implementation plans to senior executives and to one another. Discussions were heated, and a number of unit heads argued that the freedom of their units to form future strategies was constrained by the degree of competition they faced. Poor performers felt that they had little choice but to match their competitors' offerings. That hypothesis proved to be false when one of the fastest-growing units—the mobile phone business—presented its strategy canvas. Not only did the unit have a distinctive value curve, but it also faced the most intense competition. Samsung Electronics has institutionalized the use of the strategy canvas in its key business creation decisions by establishing the Value Innovation Program (VIP) Center in 1998. Core crossfunctional team members of its various business units come together in the VIP Center to discuss their strategic projects. These discussions typically focus on strategy canvases. With the value innovation knowledge it has developed, the center, equipped with twenty project rooms, assists the units in making their product and service offering decisions. In 2003, the center completed more than eighty strategic projects and opened more than ten VIP branches to meet business units' rising demands. For example, the world's leading forty-inch LCD TV, launched in December 2002, is the result of one project team's devoted four-month efforts made at the center. So is the world's bestselling mobile phone, the SGH T-100, which has sold more than ten million units. Since 1999, Samsung Electronics has established an annual Value Innovation corporate conference presided over by all of its top executives. At this conference, Samsung's hit Value Innovation projects are shared through presentations and exhibitions, and awards are given to the best cases. This is one way that Samsung Electronics establishes a common language system, instilling a corporate culture and strategic norms that drive its corporate business portfolio from red to blue oceans.7 Do your business unit heads lack an understanding of the other businesses in your corporate portfolio? Are your strategic best practices poorly communicated across your business units? Are your low-performing units quick to blame their competitive situations for their results? If the answer to any of these questions is yes, try drawing, and then sharing, the strategy canvases of your business units. Using the Pioneer-Migrator-Settler (PMS) Map Visualizing strategy can also help managers responsible for corporate strategy predict and plan the company's future growth and profit. All the companies that created blue oceans in our study have been pioneers in their industries, not necessarily in developing new technologies but in pushing the value they offer customers to new frontiers. Extending the pioneer metaphor can provide a useful way of talking about the growth potential of current and future businesses. A company's pioneers are the businesses that offer unprecedented value. These are your blue ocean strategists, and they are the most powerful sources of profitable growth. These businesses have a mass following of customers. Their value curve diverges from the competition on the strategy canvas. At the other extreme are settlers—businesses whose value curves conform to the basic shape of the industry's. These are me-too businesses. Settlers will not generally contribute much to a company's future growth. They are stuck within the red ocean. The potential of migrators lies somewhere in between. Such businesses extend the industry's curve by giving customers more for less, but they don't alter its basic shape. These businesses offer improved value, but not innovative value. These are businesses whose strategies fall on the margin between red oceans and blue oceans. A useful exercise for a corporate management team pursuing profitable growth is to plot the company's current and planned portfolios on a pioneer-migrator-settler (PMS) map. For the purpose of the exercise, settlers are defined as me-too businesses, migrators are business offerings better than most in the marketplace, and pioneers are the only ones with a mass following of customers. If both the current portfolio and the planned offerings consist mainly of settlers, the company has a low growth trajectory, is largely confined to red oceans, and needs to push for value innovation. Although the company might be profitable today as its settlers are still making money, it may well have fallen into the trap of competitive benchmarking, imitation, and intense price competition. If current and planned offerings consist of a lot of migrators, reasonable growth can be expected. But the company is not exploiting its potential for growth, and it risks being marginalized by a company that value-innovates. In our experience the more an industry is populated by settlers, the greater is the opportunity to value-innovate and create a blue ocean of new market space. This exercise is especially valuable for managers who want to see beyond today's performance. Revenue, profitability, market share, and customer satisfaction are all measures of a company's current position. Contrary to what conventional strategic thinking suggests, those measures cannot point the way to the future; changes in the environment are too rapid. Today's market share is a reflection of how well a business has performed historically. Think of the strategic reversal and market share upset that occurred when CNN entered the U.S. news market. ABC, CBS, and NBC—all with historically strong market shares—were devastated. Chief executives should instead use value and innovation as the important parameters for managing their portfolio of businesses. They should use innovation because, without it, companies are stuck in the trap of competitive improvements. They should use value because innovative ideas will be profitable only if they are linked to what buyers are willing to pay for. Clearly, what senior executives should be doing is getting their organizations to shift the balance of their future portfolio toward pioneers. That is the path to profitable growth.

Overcoming the Limitations of Strategic Planning Managers often express discontent, either explicitly or implicitly, with existing strategic planning—the core activity of strategy. To them, strategic planning should be more about collective wisdom building than top-down or bottom-up planning. They think that it should be more conversational than solely documentation-driven, and it should be more about building the big picture than about number-crunching exercises. It should have a creative component instead of being strictly analysis-driven, and it should be more motivational, invoking willing commitment, than bargaining-driven, producing negotiated commitment. Despite this appetite for change, however, scant work exists on building a viable alternative to existing strategic planning, which is the most essential management task in the sense that almost every company in the world not only does it but often takes several grueling months each year to complete the exercise. Building the process around a picture addresses many of managers' discontents with existing strategic planning and yields much better results. As Aristotle pointed out, "The soul never thinks without an image." Drawing a strategy canvas and a PMS map is not, of course, the only part of the strategic planning process. At some stage, numbers and documents must be compiled and discussed. But we believe that the details will fall into place more easily if managers start with the big picture of how to break away from the competition. The methods of visualizing strategy proposed here will put strategy back into strategic planning, and they will greatly improve your chances of creating a blue ocean. How do you maximize the size of the blue ocean you are creating? The following chapter addresses that precise question.

CHAPTER EIGHT

Reach Beyond Existing Demand

NO COMPANY WANTS to venture beyond red oceans only to find itself in a puddle. The question is, How do you maximize the size of the blue ocean you are creating? This brings us to the third principle of blue ocean strategy: Reach beyond existing demand. This is a key component of achieving value innovation. By aggregating the greatest demand for a new offering, this approach attenuates the scale risk associated with creating a new market. To achieve this, companies should challenge two conventional strategy practices. One is the focus on existing customers. The other is the drive for finer segmentation to accommodate buyer differences. Typically, to grow their share of a market, companies strive to retain and expand existing customers. This often leads to finer segmentation and greater tailoring of offerings to better meet customer preferences. The more intense the competition is, the greater, on average, is the resulting customization of offerings. As companies compete to embrace customer preferences through finer segmentation, they often risk creating too-small target markets.To maximize the size of their blue oceans, companies need to take a reverse course. Instead of concentrating on customers, they need to look to noncustomers. And instead of focusing on customer differences, they need to build on powerful commonalities in what buyers value. That allows companies to reach beyond existing demand to unlock a new mass of customers that did not exist before. Think of Callaway Golf. It aggregated new demand for its offering by looking to noncustomers. While the U.S. golf industry fought to win a greater share of existing customers, Callaway created a blue ocean of new demand by asking why sports enthusiasts and people in the country club set had not taken up golf as a sport. By looking to why people shied away from golf, it found one key commonality uniting the mass of noncustomers: Hitting the golf ball was perceived as too difficult. The small size of the golf club head demanded enormous hand-eye coordination, took time to master, and required concentration. As a result, fun was sapped for novices, and it took too long to get good at the sport. This understanding gave Callaway insight into how to aggregate new demand for its offering. The answer was Big Bertha, a golf club with a large head that made it far easier to hit the golf ball. Big Bertha not only converted noncustomers of the industry into customers, but it also pleased existing golf customers, making it a runaway bestseller across the board. With the exception of pros, it turned out that the mass of existing customers also had been frustrated with the difficulty of advancing their game by mastering the skills needed to hit the ball consistently. The club's large head also lessened this difficulty. Interestingly, however, existing customers, unlike noncustomers, had implicitly accepted the difficulty of the game. Although the mass of existing customers didn't like it, they had taken for granted that that was the way the game was played. Instead of registering their dissatisfaction with golf club makers, they themselves accepted the responsibility to improve. By looking to noncustomers and focusing on their key commonalities—not differences—Call away saw how to aggregate new demand and offer the mass of customers and noncustomers a leap in value. Where is your locus of attention—on capturing a greater share of existing customers, or on converting noncustomers of the industry into new demand? Do you seek out key commonalities in what buyers value, or do you strive to embrace customer differences through finer customization and segmentation? To reach beyond existing demand, think noncustomers before customers; commonalities before differences; and desegmentation before pursuing finer segmentation. The Three Tiers of Noncustomers Although the universe of noncustomers typically offers big blue ocean opportunities, few companies have keen insight into who noncustomers are and how to unlock them. To convert this huge latent demand into real demand in the form of thriving new customers, companies need to deepen their understanding of the universe of noncustomers. There are three tiers of noncustomers that can be transformed into customers. They differ in their relative distance from your market. the first tier of noncustomers is closest to your market. They sit on the edge of the market. They are buyers who minimally purchase an industry's offering out of necessity but are mentally noncustomers of the industry. They are waiting to jump ship and leave the industry as soon as the opportunity presents itself.

However, if offered a leap in value, not only would they stay, but also their frequency of purchases would multiply, unlocking enormous latent demand. The second tier of noncustomers is people who refuse to use your industry's offerings. These are buyers who have seen your industry's offerings as an option to fulfill their needs but have voted against them. In the Callaway case, for example, these were sports enthusiasts, especially the country club tennis set, who could have chosen golf but had consciously chosen against it. The third tier of noncustomers is farthest from your market. They are noncustomers who have never thought of your market's offerings as an option. By focusing on key commonalities across these noncustomers and existing customers, companies can understand how to pull them into their new market. Let's look at each of the three tiers of noncustomers to understand how you can attract them and expand your blue ocean. First-Tier Noncustomers These soon-to-be noncustomers are those who minimally use the current market offerings to get by as they search for something better. Upon finding any better alternative, they will eagerly jump ship. In this sense, they sit on the edge of the market. A market becomes stagnant and develops a growth problem as the number of soon-to-be noncustomers increases. Yet locked within these firsttier noncustomers is an ocean of untapped demand waiting to be released. Consider how Pret A Manger, a British fast-food chain that opened in 1988, has expanded its blue ocean by tapping into the huge latent demand of first-tier noncustomers. Before Pret, professionals in European city centers principally frequented restaurants for lunch. Sit-down restaurants offered a nice meal and setting. However, the number of first-tier noncustomers was high and rising. Growing concerns over the need for healthy eating gave people second thoughts about eating out in restaurants. And professionals did not always have time for a sit-down meal. Some restaurants were also too expensive for lunch on a daily basis. So professionals were increasingly grabbing something on the run, bringing a brown bag from home, or even skipping lunch. These first-tier noncustomers were in search of better solutions. Although there were numerous differences across them, they shared three key commonalities: They wanted lunch fast, they wanted it fresh and healthy, and they wanted it at a reasonable price. The insight gained from the commonalities across these first-tier noncustomers shed light on how Pret could unlock and aggregate untapped demand. The Pret formula is simple. It offers restaurantquality sandwiches made fresh every day from only the finest ingredients, and it makes the food available at a speed that is faster than that of restaurants and even fast food. It also delivers this in a sleek setting at reasonable prices. Consider what Pret is like. Walking into a Pret A Manger is like walking into a bright Art Deco studio. Along the walls are clean refrigerated shelves stocked with more than thirty types of sandwiches (average price $4–$6) made fresh that day, in that shop, from fresh ingredients delivered earlier that morning. People can also choose from other freshly made items, such as salads, yogurt, parfaits, blended juices, and sushi. Each store has its own kitchen, and nonfresh items are made by high-quality producers. Even in its

New York stores, Pret's baguettes are from Paris, its croissants are from Belgium, and its Danish pastries are from Denmark. And nothing is kept over to the next day. Leftover food is given to homeless shelters. In addition to offering fresh healthy sandwiches and other fresh food items, Pret speeds up the customer ordering experience from fast food's queue-order-pay-wait-receive-sit down purchasing cycle to a much faster browse-pick up-pay-leave cycle. On average, customers spend just ninety seconds from the time they get in line to the time they leave the shop. This is made possible because Pret produces ready-made sandwiches and other things at high volume with a high standardization of assembly, does not make to order, and does not serve its customers. They serve themselves as in a supermarket. Whereas sit-down restaurants have seen stagnant demand, Pret has been converting the mass of soon-to-be noncustomers into core thriving customers who eat at Pret more often than they used to eat at restaurants. Beyond this, as with Callaway, restaurant-goers who were content to eat lunch at restaurants also have been flocking to Pret. Although restaurant lunches had been acceptable, the three key commonalities of first-tier noncustomers struck a chord with these people; but unlike soon-to-be noncustomers, they had not thought to question their lunch habits. The lesson: Noncustomers tend to offer far more insight into how to unlock and grow a blue ocean than do relatively content existing customers. Today Pret A Manger sells more than twenty-five million sandwiches a year from its one hundred thirty stores in the U.K., and it recently opened stores in New York and Hong Kong. In 2002 it had sales of more than £100m ($160 million). Its growth potential triggered McDonald's to buy a 33 percent share of the company. What are the key reasons first-tier noncustomers want to jump ship and leave your industry? Look for the commonalities across their responses. Focus on these, and not on the differences between them. You will glean insight into how to desegment buyers and unleash an ocean of latent untapped demand.

Second-Tier Noncustomers These are refusing noncustomers, people who either do not use or cannot afford to use the current market offerings because they find the offerings unacceptable or beyond their means. Their needs are either dealt with by other means or ignored. Harboring within refusing noncustomers, however, is an ocean of untapped demand waiting to be released. Consider how JCDecaux, a vendor of French outdoor advertising space, pulled the mass of refusing noncustomers into its market. Before JCDecaux created a new concept in outdoor advertising called "street furniture" in 1964, the outdoor advertising industry included billboards and transport advertisement. Billboards typically were located on city outskirts and along roads where traffic quickly passed by; transport advertisement comprised panels on buses and taxies, which again people caught sight of only as they whizzed by. Outdoor advertising was not a popular campaign medium for many companies because it was viewed only in a transitory way. Outdoor ads were exposed to people for a very short time while they were in transit, and the rate of repeat visits was low. Especially for lesser-known companies, such advertising media were ineffective because they could not carry the comprehensive messages needed to introduce new names and products. Hence, many such companies refused to use such low-value-added outdoor advertising because it was either unacceptable or a luxury they could not afford. Having thought through the key commonalities that cut across refusing noncustomers of the industry, JCDecaux realized that the lack of stationary downtown locations was the key reason the industry remained unpopular and small. In searching for a solution, JCDecaux found that municipalities could offer stationary downtown locations, such as bus stops, where people tended to wait a few minutes and hence had time to read and be influenced by advertisements. JCDecaux reasoned that if it could secure these locations to use for outdoor advertising, it could convert second-tier noncustomers into customers. This gave it the idea to provide street furniture, including maintenance and upkeep, free to municipalities. JCDecaux figured that as long as the revenue generated from selling ad space exceeded the costs of providing and maintaining the furniture at an attractive profit margin, the company would be on a trajectory of strong, profitable growth. Accordingly, street furniture was created that would integrate advertising panels. In this way, JCDecaux created a breakthrough in value for second-tier noncustomers, the municipalities, and itself. The strategy eliminated cities' traditional costs associated with urban furniture. In return for free products and services, JCDecaux gained the exclusive right to display advertisements on the street furniture located in downtown areas. By making ads available in city centers, the company significantly increased the average exposure time, improving the recall capabilities of this advertising medium. The increase in exposure time also permitted richer contents and more complex messages. Moreover, as the maintainer of the urban furniture, JCDecaux could help advertisers roll out their campaigns in two to three days, as opposed to fifteen days of rollout time for traditional billboard campaigns. In response to JCDecaux's exceptional value offering, the mass of refusing noncustomers flocked to the industry. As a medium of advertisement, street furniture became the highest-growth market in the overall display advertising industry. Global spending on street furniture between 1995 and 2000, for example, grew by 60 percent compared with a 20 percent total increase in overall display advertising. By signing contracts of eight to twenty-five years with municipalities, JCDecaux gained long-term exclusive rights for displaying ads with street furniture. After an initial capital investment, the only expenditure for JCDecaux in the subsequent years was the maintenance and renewal of the furniture. The operating margin of street furniture was as high as 40 percent, compared with 14 per cent for billboards and 18 percent for transport advertisements. The exclusive contracts and high operating margins created a steady source of long-term revenue and profits. With this business model, JCDecaux was able to capture a leap in value for itself in return for a leap in value created for its buyers. Today, JCDecaux is the number one street furniture-based ad space provider worldwide, with 283,000 panels in thirty-three countries. What's more, by looking to second-tier noncustomers and focusing on the key commonalities that turned them away from the industry, JCDecaux also increased the demand for outdoor advertising by existing customers of the industry. Until then, existing customers had focused on what billboard locations or bus lines they could secure, for what period, and for how much. They took for granted that those were the only options available and worked within them. Again, it took noncustomers to shed insight into the implicit assumptions of the industry and its existing customers that could be challenged and rewritten to create a leap in value for all. What are the key reasons second-tier noncustomers refuse to use the products or services of your industry? Look for the commonalities across their responses. Focus on these, and not on their differences. You will glean insight into how to unleash an ocean of latent untapped demand. Third-Tier Noncustomers The third tier of noncustomers is the farthest away from an industry's existing customers. Typically, these unexplored noncustomers have not been targeted or thought of as potential customers by any player in the industry. That's because their needs and the business opportunities associated with them have somehow always been assumed to belong to other markets. It would drive many companies crazy to know how many thirdtier noncustomers they are forfeiting. Just think of the long-held assumption that tooth whitening was a service provided exclusively by dentists and not by oral care consumer-product companies. Consequently, oral care companies, until recently, never looked at the needs of these noncustomers. When they did, they found an ocean of latent demand waiting to be tapped; they also found that they had the capability to deliver safe, high-quality, low-cost tooth whitening solutions, and the market exploded. This potential applies to most industries. Consider the U.S. defense aerospace industry. It has been argued that the inability to control aircraft costs is a key vulnerability in the long-term military strength of the United States.1 Soaring costs combined with shrinking budgets, concluded a 1993 Pentagon report, left the military without a viable plan to replace its aging fleet of fighter aircraft.2 If the military couldn't find a way to build aircraft differently, military leaders worried, the United States would not have enough airplanes to properly defend its interests. Traditionally, the Navy, Marines, and Air Force differed in their conceptions of the ideal fighter plane and hence each branch designed and built its own aircraft independently. The Navy argued for a durable aircraft that would survive the stress of landing on carrier decks. The Marines wanted an expeditionary aircraft capable of short takeoffs and landings. The Air Force wanted the fastest and most sophisticated aircraft. Historically, these differences among the independent branches were taken for granted, and the defense aerospace industry was regarded as having three distinct and separate segments. The Joint Strike Fighter (JSF) program challenged this industry practice.3 It looked to all three segments as potentially unexplored noncustomers that could be aggregated into a new market of higher-performing, lower-cost fighter planes. Rather than accept the existing segmentation and develop products according to the differences in specifications and features demanded by each branch of the military, the JSF program questioned these differences. It searched for the key commonalities across the three branches that had previously disregarded one another. This process revealed that the two highest-cost components of the three branches' aircraft were the same: avionics (software) and engines. The shared use and production of these components held the promise of enormous cost reductions. Moreover, even though each branch had a long list of highly customized requirements, most aircraft across branches performed the same missions. The JSF team looked to understand how many of these highly customized features decisively influenced the branches' purchase decision. Interestingly, the Navy's answer did not hinge on a wide range of factors. Instead, it boiled down to only two: durability and maintainability. With aircraft stationed on aircraft carriers thousands of miles away from the nearest maintenance hangar, the Navy wants a fighter that is easy to maintain and yet durable as a Mack truck so that it can absorb the shock of carrier landings and constant exposure to salt air. Fearing that these two essential qualities would be compromised with the requirements of the Marines and the Air Force, the Navy bought its aircraft separately. The Marines had many differences in requirements from those of the other branches, but again only two kept them from decisively avoiding joint aircraft purchases: the need for short takeoff vertical landing (STOVL) and robust countermeasures. To support troops in remote and hostile conditions the Marines need an aircraft that performs as a jet fighter and yet hovers like a helicopter. And given the low-altitude, expeditionary nature of their missions, the Marines want an aircraft equipped with various countermeasures—flares, electronic jamming devices—to evade enemy groundto-air missiles because their planes are relatively easier targets given their short air-to-ground range. Tasked with maintaining global air superiority, the Air Force demands the fastest aircraft and superior tactical agility—the ability to outmaneuver all current and future enemy aircraft—and one equipped with stealth technology: radar-absorbing materials and structures to make it less visible to radar and therefore more likely to evade enemy missiles and aircraft. The other two branches' aircraft lacked these factors, and hence the Air Force had not considered them. These findings on unexplored noncustomers made the JSF a feasible project. The aim was to build one aircraft for all three divisions by combining those key factors while reducing or eliminating everything else—that is, all the factors that had been taken for granted by each branch but provided little value, or factors that had been overdesigned in the race to beat the competition. As outlined in figure 5-2, some twenty competing factors in the Marine, Navy, and Air Force segments were eliminated or reduced. By combining the factors in this way and reducing or eliminating the rest, the JSF program is able to build one aircraft for all three branches. The result is a dramatic drop in costs and hence the price per aircraft, with a leap in value in performance for all three branches. Specifically, the JSF promised to reduce costs to $33 million per aircraft from the current $190 million. At the same time, the performance of the JSF, now called the F-35, promised to be superior to that of any of the top-performing aircraft for the three branches: the Air Force's F-22, the Marine's AV-8B Harrier jet, and the Navy's F-18. Figure 5-3 illustrates how the JSF creates exceptional value by offering superior performance at lower costs. As revealed in the figure, the strategy canvas shows that while the JSF roughly maintains the distinctive strengths of the Air Force's aircraft—agility and stealth—it also offers greater maintainability, durability, countermeasures, and STOVL, the key strengths required by the Navy and the Marines. These factors are powerful additions that the Air Force had assumed it could not have. By focusing on these key decisive factors and dropping or reducing all other factors in the three dominant domains of customization— namely, design, weapons, and mission customization—the JSF program was able to offer a superior fighter plane at a lower cost By reaching beyond the existing customers of each of the three military branches, the JSF aggregated demand previously divided among them. In fall 2001, Lockheed Martin was awarded the massive $200 billion JSF contract—the largest military contract in history—over Boeing. The first JSF F-35 is set to be delivered in 2010. To date, the Pentagon is confident that the program will be an unqualified success, not only because the strategic profile of the JSF F-35 achieves exceptional value but also, equally important, because it has won the support of all three defense branches.4 Go for the Biggest Catchment There is no hard-and-fast rule to suggest which tier of noncustomers you should focus on and when. Because the scale of blue ocean opportunities that a specific tier of noncustomers can unlock varies across time and industries, you should focus on the tier that represents the biggest catchment at the time. But you should also explore whether there are overlapping commonalities across all three tiers of noncustomers. In that way, you can expand the scope of latent demand you can unleash. When that is the case, you should not focus on a specific tier but instead should look across tiers. The rule here is to go for the largest catchment. The natural strategic orientation of many companies is toward retaining existing customers and seeking further segmentation opportunities. This is especially true in the face of competitive pressure. Although this might be a good way to gain a focused competitive advantage and increase share of the existing market space, it is not likely to produce a blue ocean that expands the market and creates new demand. The point here is not to argue that it's wrong to focus on existing customers or segmentation but rather to challenge these existing, taken-for-granted strategic orientations. What we suggest is that to maximize the scale of your blue ocean you should first reach beyond existing demand to noncustomers and desegmentation opportunities as you formulate future strategies. If no such opportunities can be found, you can then move on to further exploit differences among existing customers. But in making such a strategic move, you should be aware that you might end up landing in a smaller space. You should also be aware that when your competitors succeed in attracting the mass of noncustomers with a value innovation move, many of your existing customers may be attracted away because they too may be willing to put their differences aside to gain the offered leap in value. It is not enough to maximize the size of the blue ocean you are creating. You must profit from it to create a sustainable win-win outcome. The next chapter shows how to build a viable business model that produces and maintains profitable growth for your blue ocean offering.

Get the Strategic Sequence Right

YOU'VE LOOKED ACROSS PATHS to discover possible blue oceans. You've constructed a strategy canvas that clearly articulates your future blue ocean strategy. And you have explored how to aggregate the largest possible mass of buyers for your idea. The next challenge is to build a robust business model to ensure that you make a healthy profit on your blue ocean idea. This brings us to the fourth principle of blue ocean strategy: Get the strategic sequence right. This chapter discusses the strategic sequence of fleshing out and validating blue ocean ideas to ensure their commercial viability. With an understanding of the right strategic sequence and of how to assess blue ocean ideas along the key criteria in that sequence, you dramatically reduce business model risk. The Right Strategic Sequence , companies need to build their blue ocean strategy in the sequence of buyer utility, price, cost, and adoption The starting point is buyer utility. Does your offering unlock exceptional utility? Is there a compelling reason for the mass of people to buy it? Absent this, there is no blue ocean potential to begin with. Here there are only two options. Park the idea, or rethink it until you reach an affirmative answer. When you clear the exceptional utility bar, you advance to the second step: setting the right strategic price. Remember, a company does not want to rely solely on price to create demand. The key question here is this: Is your offering priced to attract the mass of target buyers so that they have a compelling ability to pay for your offering? If it is not, they cannot buy it. Nor will the offering create irresistible market buzz. These first two steps address the revenue side of a company's business model. They ensure that you create a leap in net buyer value, where net buyer value equals the utility buyers receive minus the price they pay for it. Securing the profit side brings us to the third element: cost. Can you produce your offering at the target cost and still earn a healthy profit margin? Can you profit at the strategic price—the price easily accessible to the mass of target buyers? You should not let costs drive prices. Nor should you scale down utility because high costs block your ability to profit at the strategic price. When the target cost cannot be met, you must either forgo the idea because the blue ocean won't be profitable, or you must innovate your business model to hit the target cost. The cost side of a company's business model ensures that it creates a leap in value for itself in the form of profit—that is, the price of the offering minus the cost of production. It is the combination of exceptional utility, strategic pricing, and target costing that allows companies to achieve value innovation—a leap in value for both buyers and companies. The last step is to address adoption hurdles. What are the adoption hurdles in rolling out your idea? Have you addressed these up front? The formulation of blue ocean strategy is complete only when you can address adoption hurdles in the beginning to ensure the successful actualization of your idea. Adoption hurdles include, for example, potential resistance to the idea by retailers or partners. Because blue ocean strategies represent a significant departure from red oceans, it is key to address adoption hurdles up front. How can you assess whether your blue ocean strategy is passing through each of the four sequential steps? And how can you refine your idea to pass each bar? Let's address these questions, starting with utility. Testing for Exceptional Utility The need to assess the buyer utility of your offering may seem selfevident. Yet many companies fail to deliver exceptional value because they are obsessed by the novelty of their product or service, especially if new technology plays a part in it. Consider Philips' CD-i, an engineering marvel that failed to offer people a compelling reason to buy it. The player was promoted as the "Imagination Machine" because of its diverse functions. CD-i was a video machine, music system, game player, and teaching tool all wrapped into one. Yet it did so many different tasks that people could not understand how to use it. In addition, it lacked attractive software titles. So even though the CD-i theoretically could do almost anything, in reality it could do very little. Customers lacked a compelling reason to use it, and sales never took off. Managers responsible for Philips' CD-i (as well as Motorola's Iridium) fell into the same trap: They reveled in the bells and whistles of their new technology. They acted on the assumption that bleeding-edge technology is equivalent to bleeding-edge utility for buyers—something that, our research found, is rarely the case. The technology trap that snagged Philips and

Motorola trips up the best and brightest companies time and again. Unless the technology makes buyers' lives dramatically simpler, more convenient, more productive, less risky, or more fun and fashionable, it will not attract the masses no matter how many awards it wins. Think, for example, of Starbucks, Cirque du Soleil, The Home Depot, Southwest Airlines, [yellow tail], or Ralph Lauren: Value innovation is not the same as technology innovation. To get around this trap, the starting point, as articulated in chapter 2, is to create a strategic profile that passes the initial lit mus test of being focused, being divergent, and having a compelling tagline that speaks to buyers. Having done this, companies are ready to expressly assess where and how the new product or service will change the lives of its buyers. Such a difference in perspective is important because it means that the way a product or service is developed becomes less a function of its technical possibilities and more a function of its utility to buyers.

The Six Stages of the Buyer Experience Cycle A buyer's experience can usually be broken into a cycle of six stages, running more or less sequentially from purchase to disposal. Each stage encompasses a wide variety of specific experiences. Purchasing, for example, may include the experience of browsing eBay as well as the aisles of The Home Depot. At each stage, managers can ask a set of questions to gauge the quality of buyers' experience, as described in figure 6-3. The Six Utility Levers Cutting across the stages of the buyer's experience are what we call utility levers: the ways in which companies can unlock exceptional utility for buyers. Most of the levers are obvious. Simplicity, fun and image, and environmental friendliness need little explanation. Nor does the idea that a product might reduce a customer's financial, physical, or credibility risks. And a product or service offers convenience simply by being easy to obtain, use, or dispose of. The most commonly used lever is that of customer productivity, in which an offering helps a customer do things faster or better. To test for exceptional utility, companies should check whether their offering has removed the greatest blocks to utility across the entire buyer experience cycle for customers and noncustomers. The greatest blocks to utility often represent the greatest and most pressing opportunities to unlock exceptional value. Figure 6-4 shows how a company can identify the most compelling hot spots to unlock exceptional utility. By locating your proposed offering on the thirty-six spaces of the buyer utility map, you can clearly see how, and whether, the new idea not only creates a different utility proposition from existing offerings but also removes the biggest blocks to utility that stand in the way of converting noncustomers into customers. If your offering falls on the same space or spaces as those of other players, chances are it is not a blue ocean offering.

Consider the Ford Model T. Before its debut, the more than five hundred automakers in the United States focused on building custom-made luxury autos for the wealthy. In terms of the buyer utility map, the entire industry focused on image in the use phase, creating luxury cars for fashionable weekend outings. Only one of the thirty-six utility spaces was occupied. The greatest blocks to utility for the mass of people, however, were not in refining the auto's luxury or stylish image. Rather, they had to do with two other factors. One was convenience in the use phase. The bumpy and muddy dirt roads that prevailed at the century's start were a natural for horses to tread over but often prevented finely crafted autos from passing. This significantly limited where and when cars could travel (driving on rainy and snowy days was ill advised), making the use of the car limited and inconvenient. The second block to utility was risk in the maintenance phase. The cars, being finely crafted and having multiple options, often broke down, requiring experts to fix them, and experts were expensive and in short supply .

In one fell swoop, Ford's Model T eliminated these two utility blocks. The Model T was called the car for the great multitude. It came in only one color (black) and one model, with scant options. In this way, Ford eliminated investments in image in the use phase. Instead of creating cars for weekends in the countryside—a luxury few could justify—Ford's Model T was made for everyday use. It was reliable. It was durable; it was designed to travel effortlessly over dirt roads and in rain, sleet, or shine. It was easy to fix and use. People could learn to drive it in one day. In this way the buyer utility map highlights the differences between ideas that genuinely create new and exceptional utility and those that are essentially revisions of existing offerings or technological breakthroughs not linked to value. The aim is to check whether your offering passes the exceptional utility test, as did the Model T. By applying this diagnostic, you can find out how your idea needs to be refined. Where are the greatest blocks to utility across the buyer experience cycle for your customers and noncustomers? Does your offering effectively eliminate these blocks? If it does not, chances are your offering is innovation for innovation's sake or a revision of existing offerings. When a company's offering passes this test, it is ready to move to the next step. From Exceptional Utility to Strategic Pricing To secure a strong revenue stream for your offering, you must set the right strategic price. This step ensures that buyers not only will want to buy your offering but also will have a compelling ability to pay for it. Many companies take a reverse course, first testing the waters of a new product or service by targeting novelty-seeking, price-insensitive customers at the launch of a new business idea; only over time do they drop prices to attract mainstream buyers. It is increasingly important, however, to know from the start what price will quickly capture the mass of target buyers.

There are two reasons for this change. First, companies are discovering that volume generates higher returns than it used to. As the nature of goods becomes more knowledge intensive, companies bear much more of their costs in product development than in manufacturing. This is easy to understand in the software industry. Producing the first copy of the Windows XP operating system, for example, cost Microsoft billions of dollars, whereas subsequent copies involved no more than the nearly trivial cost of a CD. This makes volume key. A second reason is that to a buyer, the value of a product or service may be closely tied to the total number of people using it. An example is the online auction service managed by eBay. People will not buy a product or service when it is used by few others. As a result of this phenomenon, called network externalities, many products and services are an all-or-nothing proposition: Either you sell millions at once, or you sell nothing at all.1 In the meantime, the rise of knowledge-intensive products also creates the potential for free riding. This relates to the nonrival and partially excludable nature of knowledge.2 The use of a rival good by one firm precludes its use by another. So, for example, Nobel Prize–winning scientists who are fully employed by IBM cannot simultaneously be employed by another company. Nor can scrap steel consumed by Nucor be simultaneously consumed for production by other minimill steel makers. In contrast, the use of a nonrival good by one firm does not limit its use by another. Ideas fall into this category. So, for example, when Virgin Atlantic Airways launched its Upper Class brand—a new concept in business-class travel that essentially combined the huge seats and legroom of traditional first class with the price of business-class tickets—other airlines were free to apply this idea to their own business-class service without limiting Virgin's ability to use it. This makes competitive imitation not only possible but less costly. The cost and risk of developing an innovative idea are borne by the initiator, not the follower. This challenge is exacerbated when the notion of excludability is considered. Excludability is a function both of the nature of the good and of the legal system. A good is excludable if the company can prevent others from using it because of, for example, limited access or patent protection. Intel, for example, can exclude other microprocessor chipmakers from using its manufacturing facilities through property ownership laws. The women's fitness club Curves, however, cannot exclude someone from walking into any of its centers, studying its layout, atmosphere, and exercise routine, and mimicking its women's fitness concept: Women need only thirty minutes, three days a week, to get in shape while having fun with other women, with none of the usual embarrassment faced at gyms. The highest value-added element of the Curves formula is not excludable. Once ideas are out there, knowledge naturally spills over to other firms. This lack of excludability reinforces the risk of free riding. Like the creative and explosive concepts of Curves, Starbucks, or Southwest Airlines, many of the most powerful blue ocean ideas have tremendous value but in themselves consist of no new technological discoveries. As a result they are neither patentable nor excludable and hence are vulnerable to imitation. All this means that the strategic price you set for your offering must not only attract buyers in large numbers but also help you to retain them. Given the high potential for free riding, an offering's reputation must be earned on day one, because brand building increasingly relies heavily on word-of-mouth recommendations spreading rapidly through our networked society. Companies must therefore start with an offer that buyers can't refuse and must keep it that way to discourage any free-riding imitations. This is what makes strategic pricing key. Strategic pricing addresses this question: Is your offering priced to attract the mass of target buyers from the start so that they have a compelling ability to pay for it? When exceptional utility is combined with strategic pricing, imitation is discouraged. We have developed a tool called the price corridor of the mass to help managers find the right price for an irresistible offer, which, by the way, isn't necessarily the lower price. The tool involves two distinct but interrelated steps.

Step 1: Identify the Price Corridor of the Mass In setting a price, all companies look first at the products and services that most closely resemble their idea in terms of form. Typically they look at other products and services within their industries. That's still a necessary exercise, of course, but it is not sufficient to attract new customers. So the main challenge in determining a strategic price is to understand the price sensitivities of those people who will be comparing the new product or service with a host of very different-looking products and services offered outside the group of traditional competitors. A good way to look outside industry boundaries is to list products and services that fall into two categories: those that take different forms but perform the same function, and those that take different forms and functions but share the same over-arching objective.

Different form, same function. Many companies that create blue oceans attract customers from other industries who use a product or service that performs the same function or bears the same core utility as the new one but takes a very different physical form. In the case of Ford's Model T, Ford looked to the horse-drawn carriage. The horse-drawn carriage had the same core utility as the car: transportation for individuals and families. But it had a very different form: a live animal versus a machine. Ford effectively converted the majority of noncustomers of the auto industry, namely customers of horse-drawn carriages, into customers of its own blue ocean by pricing its Model T against horse-drawn carriages and not the cars of other automakers. In the case of the school lunch catering industry, raising this question led to an interesting insight. Suddenly those parents who make their children's lunches came into the equation. For many children, parents had the same function: making their child's lunch. But they had a very different form: mom or dad versus a lunch line in the cafeteria. Different form and function, same objective. Some companies lure customers from even further away. Cirque du Soleil, for example, has diverted customers from a wide range of evening activities. Its growth came in part through drawing people away from other activities that differed in both form and function. For example, bars and restaurants have few physical features in common with a circus. They also serve a distinct function by providing conversational and gastronomical pleasure, a very different experience from the visual entertainment that a circus offers. Yet despite these differences in form and function, people have the same objective in undertaking these three activities: to enjoy a night out. Listing the groups of alternative products and services allows managers to see the full range of buyers they can poach from other industries as well as from nonindustries, such as parents (for the school lunch catering industry) or the noble pencil in managing household finances (for the personal finance software industry).

Having done this, managers should then graphically plot the price and volume of these alternatives, as shown in figure 6-5. This approach provides a straightforward way to identify where the mass of target buyers is and what prices these buyers are prepared to pay for the products and services they currently use. The price bandwidth that captures the largest groups of target buyers is the price corridor of the mass. In some cases, the range is very wide. For Southwest Airlines, for example, the price corridor of the mass covered the group of people paying, on average, $400 to buy an economy-class short-haul ticket to about $60 for the cost of going the same distance by car. The key here is not to pursue pricing against the competition within an industry but rather to pursue pricing against substitutes and alternatives across industries and nonindustries. Had Ford, for example, priced its Model T against other autos, which were more than three times the price of horse-drawn carriages, the market for the Model T would not have exploded. Step 2: Specify a Level Within the Price Corridor The second part of the tool helps managers determine how high a price they can afford to set within the corridor without inviting competition from imitation products or services. That assessment depends on two principal factors. First is the degree to which the product or service is protected legally through patents or copyrights. Second is the degree to which the company owns some exclusive asset or core capability, such as an expensive production plant, that can block imitation. Dyson, a British electrical white goods company, for example, has been able to charge a high unit price for its bagless vacuum cleaner since the product's launch in 1995, thanks to both strong patents and hard-to-imitate service capabilities. Many other companies have used upper-boundary strategic pricing to attract the mass of target buyers. Examples include DuPont with its Lycra brand in specialty chemicals, Philips' ALTO in the professional lighting industry, SAP in the business application software industry, and Bloomberg in the financial software industry.

On the other hand, companies with uncertain patent and asset protection should consider pricing somewhere in the middle of the corridor. As for companies that have no such protection, they must set a relatively low price. In the case of Southwest Airlines, because its service wasn't patentable and required no exclusive assets, its ticket prices fell into the lower boundary of the corridor—namely, against the price of car travel. Companies would be wise to pursue mid- to lower-boundary strategic pricing from the start if any of the following apply: • Their blue ocean offering has high fixed costs and marginal variable costs. • Their attractiveness depends heavily on network externalities. • Their cost structure benefits from steep economies of scale and scope. In these cases, volume brings with it significant cost advantages, something that makes pricing for volume even more key. The price corridor of the mass not only signals the strategic pricing zone central to pulling in an ocean of new demand but also signals how you might need to adjust your initial price estimates to achieve this. When your offering passes the test of strategic pricing, you're ready to move to the next step. From Strategic Pricing to Target Costing Target costing, the next step in the strategic sequence, addresses the profit side of the business model. To maximize the profit potential of a blue ocean idea, a company should start with the strategic price and then deduct its desired profit margin from the price to arrive at the target cost. Here, price-minus costing, and not cost-plus pricing, is essential if you are to arrive at a cost structure that is both profitable and hard for potential followers to match. When target costing is driven by strategic pricing, however, it is usually aggressive. Part of the challenge of meeting the target cost is addressed in building a strategic profile that has not only divergence but also focus, which makes a company strip out costs. Think of the cost reductions Cirque du Soleil enjoyed by eliminating animals and stars or that Ford enjoyed by making the Model T in one color and one model having few options. Sometimes these reductions are sufficient to hit the cost target, but often they are not. Consider the cost innovations that Ford had to introduce to meet its aggressive target cost for the Model T. Ford had to scrap the standard manufacturing system, in which cars were handmade by skilled craftsmen from start to finish. Instead, Ford introduced the assembly line, which replaced skilled craftsmen with ordinary unskilled laborers, who worked one small task faster and more efficiently, cutting the time to make a Model T from twenty-one days to four days and cutting labor hours by 60 percent.3 Had Ford not introduced these cost innovations, it could not have met its strategic price profitably. Instead of drilling down and finding ways to creatively meet the target cost as Ford did, if companies give in to the tempting route of either bumping up the strategic price or cutting back on utility, they are not on the path to lucrative blue waters. To hit the cost target, companies have three principal levers. The first involves streamlining operations and introducing cost innovations from manufacturing to distribution. Can the product's or service's raw materials be replaced by unconventional, less expensive ones—such as switching from metal to plastic or shifting a call center from the U.K. to Bangalore? Can high-cost, low-valueadded activities in your value chain be significantly eliminated, reduced, or outsourced? Can the physical location of your product or service be shifted from prime real estate locations to lower-cost locations, as The Home Depot, IKEA, and Wal-Mart have done in retail or Southwest Airlines has done by shifting from major to secondary airports? Can you truncate the number of parts or steps used in production by shifting the way things are made, as Ford did by introducing the assembly line? Can you digitize activities to reduce costs?

By probing questions such as these, the Swiss watch company Swatch, for example, was able to arrive at a cost structure some 30 percent lower than any other watch company in the world. At the start, Nicolas Hayek, chairman of Swatch, set up a project team to determine the strategic price for the Swatch. At the time, cheap (about $75), high-precision quartz watches from Japan and Hong Kong were capturing the mass market. Swatch set the price at $40, a price at which people could buy multiple Swatches as fashion accessories. The low price left no profit margin for Japanese or Hong Kong-based companies to copy Swatch and undercut its price. Directed to sell the Swatch for that price and not a penny more, the Swatch project team worked backwards to arrive at the target cost, a process that involved determining the margin Swatch needed to support marketing and services and earn a profit. Given the high cost of Swiss labor, Swatch was able to achieve this goal only by making radical changes in the product and production methods. Instead of using the more traditional metal or leather, for example, Swatch used plastic. Swatch's engineers also drastically simplified the design of the watch's inner workings, reducing the number of parts from one hundred fifty to fifty-one. Finally, the engineers developed new and cheaper assembly techniques; for example, the watch cases were sealed by ultrasonic welding instead of screws. Taken together, the design and manufacturing changes enabled Swatch to reduce direct labor costs from 30 percent to less than 10 percent of total costs. These cost innovations produced a cost structure that is hard to beat and let Swatch profitably dominate the mass market for watches, a market previously dominated by Asian manufacturers with a cheaper labor pool. Beyond streamlining operations and introducing cost innovations, a second lever companies can pull to meet their target cost is partnering. In bringing a new product or service to market, many companies mistakenly try to carry out all the production and distribution activities themselves. Sometimes that's because they see the product or service as a platform for developing new capabilities. Other times it is simply a matter of not considering other outside options. Partnering, however, provides a way for companies to secure needed capabilities fast and effectively while dropping their cost structure. It allows a company to leverage other companies' expertise and economies of scale. Partnering includes closing gaps in capabilities through making small acquisitions when doing so is faster and cheaper, providing access to needed expertise that has already been mastered. A large part of IKEA's ability to meet its target cost, for example, comes down to partnering. IKEA seeks out the lowest prices for materials and production via partnering with some fifteen hundred manufacturing companies in more than fifty countries to ensure it the lowest cost and fastest production of products in its IKEA lineup of some twenty thousand items. Or consider German-based, world-leading business application software maker SAP. By partnering with Oracle, SAP saved hundreds of millions if not billions of dollars in development costs and got a world-class central database, namely Oracle's, which sits at the heart of SAP's core products R/2 and R/3. SAP went a step further and also partnered with leading consulting firms, such as Capgemini and Accenture, to gain a global sales force overnight at no extra cost. Whereas Oracle had the fixed costs of a much smaller sales force on its balance sheet, SAP was able to leverage Capgemini's and Accenture's strong global networks to reach SAP's target customers, with no cost implication to the company. Sometimes, however, no amount of streamlining and cost innovation or partnering will make it possible for a company to deliver its target cost. This brings us to the third lever companies can use to make their desired profit margin without compromising their strategic price: changing the pricing model of the industry. By changing the pricing model used—and not the level of the strategic price—companies can often overcome this problem. When film videotapes first came out, for example, they were priced at around $80. Few people were willing to pay that amount because no one expected to watch the video more than two or three times. The strategic price of a video had to be set in relation to going to the movies and not to owning a tape for life. So at $80 a tape, demand was not taking off. How could a company make money by selling the videos at only a few dollars if it followed the path of using strategic pricing? The answer was that it couldn't. Blockbuster, however, got around this problem by changing the pricing model from selling to renting. This allowed it to strategically price videotapes at only a few dollars per rental. The result was that the home video market exploded and Blockbuster made more money by repeatedly renting the same $80 videos than it could have by selling them outright. Similarly, IBM exploded the tabulating market by shifting the pricing model from selling to leasing to hit its strategic price while covering its cost structure. In addition to Blockbuster's rental model or IBM's leasing model, companies have used several innovations in pricing models to profitably deliver on the strategic price. One model is the timeshare. The New Jersey company NetJets follows this model to make jets accessible to a wide range of corporate customers, who buy the right to use a jet for a certain amount of time rather than buy the jet itself. Another model is the slice-share; mutual fund managers, for example, bring high-quality portfolio services—traditionally provided by private banks to the rich—to the small investor by selling a sliver of the portfolio rather than its whole. Some companies are abandoning the concept of price altogether. Instead, they give products to customers in return for an equity interest in the customer's business. Hewlett-Packard, for example, has traded high-powered servers to Silicon Valley start-ups for a share of their revenues. The customers get immediate access to a key capability, and HP stands to earn a lot more than the price of the machine. The aim is not to compromise on the strategic price but to hit the target through a new price model. We call this pricing innovation. Remember, however, that what is a pricing innovation for one industry, such as video rentals, is often a standard pricing model in another industry.

company begins with its strategic price, from which it deducts its target profit margin to arrive at its target cost. To hit the cost target that supports that profit, companies have two key levers: One is streamlining and cost innovations, and the other is partnering. When the target cost cannot be met despite all efforts to build a low-cost business model, the company should turn to the third lever, pricing innovation, to profitably meet the strategic price. Of course, even when the target cost can be met, pricing innovation still can be pursued. When a company's offering successfully addresses the profit side of the business model, the company is ready to advance to the final step in the sequence of blue ocean strategy. A business model built in the sequence of exceptional utility, strategic pricing, and target costing produces value innovation. Unlike the practice of conventional technology innovators, value innovation is based on a win-win game among buyers, companies, and society. Appendix C, "The Market Dynamics of Value Innovation," illustrates how such a game is played out in the market and shows the economic and social welfare implications for its stakeholders. From Utility, Price, and Cost to Adoption Even an unbeatable business model may not be enough to guarantee the commercial success of a blue ocean idea. Almost by definition, it threatens the status quo, and for that reason it may provoke fear and resistance among a company's three main stakeholders: its employees, its business partners, and the general public. Before plowing forward and investing in the new idea, the company must first overcome such fears by educating the fearful. Employees Failure to adequately address the concerns of employees about the impact of a new business idea on their livelihoods can be expensive. When Merrill Lynch's management, for example, announced plans to create an online brokerage service, its stock price fell by 14 percent as reports emerged of resistance and infighting within the company's large retail brokerage division. Before companies go public with an idea, they should make a concerted effort to communicate to employees that they are aware of the threats posed by the execution of the idea. Companies should work with employees to find ways of defusing the threats so that everyone in the company wins, despite shifts in people's roles, responsibilities, and rewards. In contrast to Merrill Lynch, Morgan Stanley Dean Witter & Co. engaged employees in an open internal discussion of the company's strategy for meeting the challenge of the Internet. Morgan's efforts paid off handsomely. Because the market realized that its employees understood the need for an e-venture, the company's shares rose 13 percent when it eventually announced the venture. Business Partners Potentially even more damaging than employee disaffection is the resistance of partners who fear that their revenue streams or market positions are threatened by a new business idea. That was the problem faced by SAP when it was developing its product AcceleratedSAP (ASAP), an enterprise software system that was fast to implement and hence low cost. ASAP brought business application software within the reach of midsized and small companies for the first time. The problem was that the development of best-practice templates for ASAP required the active cooperation of large consulting firms that were deriving substantial income from lengthy implementations of SAP's other products. As a result, they were not necessarily incentivized to find the fastest way to implement the company's software. SAP resolved the dilemma by openly discussing the issues with its partners. Its executives convinced the consulting firms that they stood to gain more business by cooperating. Although ASAP would reduce implementation time for small and midsized companies, consultants would gain access to a new client base that would more than compensate for some lost revenues from larger companies. The new system would also offer consultants a way to respond to customers' increasingly vocal concerns that business application software took too long to implement. The General Public Opposition to a new business idea can also spread to the general public, especially if the idea is very new and innovative, threatening established social or political norms. The effects can be devastating. Consider Monsanto, which makes genetically modified foods. Its intentions have been questioned by European consumers, largely because of the efforts of environmental groups such as Greenpeace, Friends of the Earth, and the Soil Association. The attacks of these groups have struck many chords in Europe, which has a history of environmental concern and powerful agricultural lobbies. Monsanto's mistake was to let others take charge of the debate. The company should have educated the environmental groups as well as the public on the benefits of genetically modified food and its potential to eliminate world famine and disease. When the products came out, Monsanto should have given consumers a choice between organic and genetically modified foods by labeling which products had genetically modified seeds as their base. If Monsanto had taken these steps, then instead of being vilified, it might have ended up as the "Intel Inside" of food for the future—the provider of the essential technology.

CHAPTER TEN

Organizational Hurdles

The challenge of execution exists, of course, for any strategy. Companies, like individuals, often have a tough time translating thought into action whether in red or blue oceans. But compared with red ocean strategy, blue ocean strategy represents a significant departure from the status quo. It hinges on a shift from convergence to divergence in value curves at lower costs. That raises the execution bar. Managers have assured us that the challenge is steep. They face four hurdles. One is cognitive: waking employees up to the need for a strategic shift. Red oceans may not be the paths to future profitable growth, but they feel comfortable to people and may have even served an organization well until now, so why rock the boat? The second hurdle is limited resources. The greater the shift in strategy, the greater it is assumed are the resources needed to execute it. But resources were being cut, and not raised, in many of the organizations we studied.Third is motivation. How do you motivate key players to move fast and tenaciously to carry out a break from the status quo? That will take years, and managers don't have that kind of time. The final hurdle is politics. As one manager put it, "In our organization you get shot down before you stand up." Although all companies face different degrees of these hurdles, and many may face only some subset of the four, knowing how to triumph over them is key to attenuating organizational risk. This brings us to the fifth principle of blue ocean strategy: Overcome key organizational hurdles to make blue ocean strategy happen in action. To achieve this effectively, however, companies must abandon perceived wisdom on effecting change. Conventional wisdom asserts that the greater the change, the greater the resources and time you will need to bring about results. Instead, you need to flip conventional wisdom on its head using what we call tipping point leadership. Tipping point leadership allows you to overcome these four hurdles fast and at low cost while winning employees' backing in executing a break from the status quo. Tipping Point Leadership in Action Consider the New York City Police Department (NYPD), which executed a blue ocean strategy in the 1990s in the public sector. When Bill Bratton was appointed police commissioner of New York City in February 1994, the odds were stacked against him to an extent few executives ever face. In the early 1990s, New York City was veering toward anarchy. Murders were at an all-time high. Muggings, Mafia hits, vigilantes, and armed robberies filled the daily headlines. New Yorkers were under siege. But Bratton's budget was frozen. Indeed, after three decades of mounting crime in New York City, many social scientists had concluded that it was impervious to police intervention. The citizens of New York City were crying out. A front-page headline in the New York Post had screamed: "Dave do something!"—a direct call to then mayor David Dinkins to get crime down fast.1 With miserable pay, dangerous workingconditions, long hours, and little hope of advancement in a tenure promotion system, morale among the NYPD's thirty-six thousand officers was at rock bottom—not to mention the debilitating effects of budget cuts, dilapidated equipment, and corruption. In business terms, the NYPD was a cash-strapped organization with thirty-six thousand employees wedded to the status quo, unmotivated, and underpaid; a disgruntled customer base—New York City's citizens; and rapidly declining performance as measured by the increase in crime, fear, and disorder. Entrenched turf wars and politics topped off the cake. In short, leading the NYPD to execute a shift in strategy was a managerial nightmare far beyond the imaginations of most executives. The competition—the criminals—was strong and rising. Yet in less than two years and without an increase in his budget, Bratton turned New York City into the safest large city in the United States. He broke out of the red ocean with a blue ocean policing strategy that revolutionized U.S. policing as it was then known. Between 1994 and 1996, the organization won as "profits" jumped: Felony crime fell 39 percent, murders 50 percent, and theft 35 percent. "Customers" won: Gallup polls reported that public confidence in the NYPD leaped from 37 percent to 73 percent. And employees won: Internal surveys showed job satisfaction in the NYPD reaching an all-time high. As one patrolman put it, "We would have marched to hell and back for that guy." Perhaps most impressively, the changes have outlasted its leader, implying a fundamental shift in the organizational culture and strategy of the NYPD. Even after Bratton's departure in 1996, crime rates have continued to fall. Few corporate leaders face organizational hurdles as steep as Bratton did in executing a break from the status quo. And still fewer are able to orchestrate the type of performance leap that Bratton achieved under any organizational conditions, let alone those as stringent as he encountered. Even Jack Welch needed some ten years and tens of millions of dollars of restructuring and training to turn GE into a powerhouse. Moreover, defying conventional wisdom, Bratton achieved these breakthrough results in record time with scarce resources while lifting employee morale, creating a win-win for all involved. Nor was this Bratton's first strategic reversal. It was his fifth, with each of the others also achieved despite his facing all four hurdles that managers consistently claim limit their ability to execute blue ocean strategy: the cognitive hurdle that blinds employees from seeing that radical change is necessary; the resource hurdle that is endemic in firms; the motivational hurdle that discourages and demoralizes staff; and the political hurdle of internal and external resistance to change.

Tipping point leadership builds on the rarely exploited corporate reality that in every organization, there are people, acts, and activities that exercise a disproportionate influence on performance. Hence, contrary to conventional wisdom, mounting a massive challenge is not about putting forth an equally massive response where performance gains are achieved by proportional investments in time and resources. Rather, it is about conserving resources and cutting time by focusing on identifying and then leveraging the factors of disproportionate influence in an organization. The key questions answered by tipping point leaders are as follows: What factors or acts exercise a disproportionately positive influence on breaking the status quo? On getting the maximum bang out of each buck of resources? On motivating key players to aggressively move forward with change? And on knocking down political roadblocks that often trip up even the best strategies? By singlemindedly focusing on points of disproportionate influence, tipping point leaders can topple the four hurdles that limit execution of blue ocean strategy. They can do this fast and at low cost. Let us consider how you can leverage disproportionate influence factors to tip all four hurdles to move from thought to action in the execution of blue ocean strategy. Break Through the Cognitive Hurdle In many turnarounds and corporate transformations, the hardest battle is simply to make people aware of the need for a strategic shift and to agree on its causes. Most CEOs will try to make the case for change simply by pointing to the numbers and insisting that the company set and achieve better results: "There are only two performance alternatives: to make the performance targets or to beat them."But as we all know, figures can be manipulated. Insisting on stretch goals encourages abuse in the budgetary process. This, in turn, creates hostility and suspicion between the various parts of an organization. Even when the numbers are not manipulated, they can mislead. Salespeople on commission, for example, are seldom sensitive to the costs of the sales they produce. What's more, messages communicated through numbers seldom stick with people. The case for change feels abstract and removed from the sphere of the line managers, who are the very people the CEO needs to win over. Those whose units are doing well feel that the criticism is not directed at them; the problem is top management's. Meanwhile, managers of poorly performing units feel that they are being put on notice, and people who are worried about personal job security are more likely to scan the job market than to try to solve the company's problems. Tipping point leadership does not rely on numbers to break through the organization's cognitive hurdle. To tip the cognitive hurdle fast, tipping point leaders such as Bratton zoom in on the act of disproportionate influence: making people see and experience harsh reality firsthand. Research in neuroscience and cognitive science shows that people remember and respond most effectively to what they see and experience: "Seeing is believing." In the realm of experience, positive stimuli reinforce behavior, whereas negative stimuli change attitudes and behavior. Simply put, if a child puts a finger in icing and tastes it, the better it tastes the more the child will taste it repetitively. No parental advice is needed to encourage that behavior. Conversely, after a child puts a finger on a burning stove, he or she will never do it again. After a negative experience, children will change their behavior of their own accord; again, no parental pestering is required.3 On the other hand, experiences that don't involve touching, seeing, or feeling actual results, such as being presented with an abstract sheet of numbers, are shown to be non-impactful and easily forgotten.4 Tipping point leadership builds on this insight to inspire a fast change in mindset that is internally driven of people's own accord. Instead of relying on numbers to tip the cognitive hurdle, they make people experience the need for change in two ways. Ride the "Electric Sewer" To break the status quo, employees must come face-to-face with the worst operational problems. Don't let top brass, middle brass, or any brass hypothesize about reality. Numbers are disputable and uninspiring, but coming face-to-face with poor performance is shocking and inescapable, but actionable. This direct experience exercises a disproportionate influence on tipping people's cognitive hurdle fast. Consider this example. In the 1990s the New York subway system reeked of fear, so much so that it earned the epithet "electric sewer." Revenues were tumbling fast as citizens boycotted the system. But members of the New York City Transit Police department were in denial. Why? Only 3 percent of the city's major crimes happened on the subway. So no matter how much the public cried out, their cries fell on deaf ears. There was no perceived need to rethink police strategies. Then Bratton was appointed chief, and in a matter of weeks he orchestrated a complete break from the status quo in the mindset of the city's police. How? Not by force, nor by arguing for numbers, but by making top brass and middle brass—starting with himself— ride the electric sewer day and night. Until Bratton came along, that had not been done. Although the statistics may have told the police that the subway was safe, what they now saw was what every New Yorker faced every day: a subway system on the verge of anarchy. Gangs of youths patrolled the cars, people jumped turnstiles, and the riders faced graffiti, aggressive begging, and winos sprawled over benches. The police could no longer evade the ugly truth. No one could argue that current police strategies didn't require a substantial departure from the status quo—and fast. Showing the worst reality to your superiors can also shift their mindset fast. A similar approach works to help sensitize superiors to a leader's needs fast. Yet few leaders exploit the power of this rapid wake-up call. Rather, they do the opposite. They try to garner support based on a numbers case that lacks urgency and emotional impetus. Or they try to put forth the most exemplary case of their operational excellence to garner support. Although these alternatives may work, neither leads to tipping superiors' cognitive hurdle as fast and stunningly as showing the worst. When Bratton, for example, was running the police division of the Massachusetts Bay Transportation Authority (MBTA), the MBTA board decided to purchase small squad cars that would be cheaper to buy and to run. That went against Bratton's new policing strategy. Instead of fighting the decision, however, or arguing for a larger budget—something that would have taken months to reevaluate and probably would have been rejected in the end— Bratton invited the MBTA's general manager for a tour of his unit to see the district. To let the general manager see the horror he was trying to rectify, Bratton picked him up in a small car just like the ones that were being ordered. He jammed the seats up front to let the manager feel how little legroom a six-foot cop would get, and then Bratton drove over every pothole he could. Bratton also put on his belt, cuffs, and gun for the trip so that the manager would see how little space there was for the tools of the police officer's trade. After two hours, the general manager wanted out. He told Bratton he didn't know how Bratton could stand being in such a cramped car for so long on his own, never mind having a criminal in the back seat. Bratton got the larger cars his new strategy demanded. Meet with Disgruntled Customers To tip the cognitive hurdle, not only must you get your managers out of the office to see operational horror, but also you must get them to listen to their most disgruntled customers firsthand. Don't rely on market surveys. To what extent does your top team actively observe the market firsthand and meet with your most disgruntled customers to hear their concerns? Do you ever wonder why sales don't match your confidence in your product? Simply put, there is no substitute for meeting and listening to dissatisfied customers directly. In the late 1970s, Boston's Police District 4, which housed the Symphony Hall, Christian Science Mother Church, and other cultural institutions, was experiencing a serious surge in crime. The public was increasingly intimidated; residents were selling their homes and leaving, thereby pushing the community into a downward spiral. But even though the citizens were leaving the area in droves, the police force under Bratton's direction felt they were doing a fine job. The performance indicators they historically used to benchmark themselves against other police departments were tip-top: 911 response times were down, and felony crime arrests were up. To solve the paradox Bratton arranged a series of town hall meetings between his officers and the neighborhood residents. It didn't take long to find the gap in perceptions. Although the police officers took great pride in short response times and their record in solving major crimes, these efforts went unnoticed and unappreciated by citizens; few felt endangered by large-scale crimes. What they felt victimized by and harassed by were the constant minor irritants: winos, panhandlers, prostitutes, and graffiti. The town meetings led to a complete overhaul of police priorities to focus on the blue ocean strategy of "broken windows."5 Crime went down, and the neighborhood felt safe again. When you want to wake up your organization to the need for a strategic shift and a break from the status quo, do you make your case with numbers? Or do you get your managers, employees, and superiors (and yourself) face-to-face with your worst operational problems? Do you get your managers to meet the market and listen to disenchanted customers holler? Or do you outsource your eyes and send out market research questionnaires?

Jump the Resource Hurdle After people in an organization accept the need for a strategic shift and more or less agree on the contours of the new strategy, most leaders are faced with the stark reality of limited resources. Do they have the money to spend on the necessary changes? At this point, most reformist CEOs do one of two things. Either they trim their ambitions and demoralize their work force all over again, or they fight for more resources from their bankers and shareholders, a process that can take time and divert attention from the underlying problems. That's not to say that this approach is not necessary or worthwhile, but acquiring more resources is often a long, politically charged process. How do you get an organization to execute a strategic shift with fewer resources? Instead of focusing on getting more resources, tipping point leaders concentrate on multiplying the value of the resources they have. When it comes to scarce resources, there are three factors of disproportionate influence that executives can leverage to dramatically free resources, on the one hand, and multiply the value of resources, on the other. These are hot spots, cold spots, and horse trading. Hot spots are activities that have low resource input but high potential performance gains. In contrast, cold spots are activities that have high resource input but low performance impact. In every organization, hot spots and cold spots typically abound. Horse trading involves trading your unit's excess resources in one area for another unit's excess resources to fill remaining resource gaps. By learning to use their current resources right, companies often find they can tip the resource hurdle outright. What actions consume your greatest resources but have scant performance impact? Conversely, what activities have the greatest performance impact but are resource starved? When the questions are framed in this way, organizations rapidly gain insight into freeing up low-return resources and redirecting them to high-impact areas. In this way, both lower costs and higher value are simultaneously pursued and achieved. Redistribute Resources to Your Hot Spots At the New York Transit Police, Bratton's predecessors argued that to make the city's subways safe they had to have an officer ride every subway line and patrol every entrance and exit. To increase profits (lower crime) would mean increasing costs (police officers) in multiples that were not possible given the budget. The underlying logic was that increments in performance could be achieved only with proportional increments in resources—the same inherent logic guiding most companies' view of performance gains. Bratton, however, achieved the sharpest drop in subway crime, fear, and disorder in Transit's history, not with more police officers but with police officers targeted at hot spots. His analysis revealed that although the subway system was a maze of lines and entrances and exits, the vast majority of crimes occurred at only a few stations and on a few lines. He also found that these hot spots were starved for police attention even though they exercised a disproportionate impact on crime performance, whereas lines and stations that almost never reported criminal activity were staffed equally. The solution was a complete refocusing of cops at subway hot spots to overwhelm the criminal element. And crime came tumbling down while the size of the police force remained constant. Similarly, before Bratton's arrival at the NYPD the narcotics unit worked nine-to-five weekday-only shifts and made up less than 5 percent of the department's human resources. To search out resource hot spots, in one of his initial meetings with the NYPD's chiefs Bratton's deputy commissioner of crime strategy, Jack Maple, asked people around the table for their estimates of the percentage of crimes attributable to narcotics usage. Most said 50 percent, others 70 percent; the lowest estimate was 30 percent. On that basis, as Maple pointed out, it was hard to argue that a narcotics unit consisting of less than 5 percent of the NYPD force was not grossly understaffed. What's more, it turned out that the narcotics squad largely worked Monday to Friday, even though most drugs were sold over the weekend, when drug-related crimes persistently occurred. Why? That was the way it had always been; it was the unquestioned modus operandi. When these facts were presented and the hot spot identified, Bratton's case for a major reallocation of staff and resources within the NYPD was quickly accepted. Accordingly, Bratton reallocated staff and resources on the hot spot, and drug crime plummeted. Where did he get the resources to do this? He simultaneously assessed his organization's cold spots. Redirect Resources from Your Cold Spots Leaders need to free up resources by searching out cold spots. Again in the subway, Bratton found that one of the biggest cold spots was processing criminals in court. On average, it would take an officer sixteen hours to take someone downtown to process even the pettiest of crimes. This was time officers were not patrolling the subway and adding value. Bratton changed all that. Instead of bringing criminals to the court, he brought processing centers to the criminals by using "bust buses"—roving old buses retrofitted into miniature police stations that were parked outside subway stations. Now instead of dragging a suspect down to the courthouse across town, a police officer needed only escort the suspect up to street level to the bus. This cut processing time from sixteen hours to just one, freeing more officers to patrol the subway and catch criminals. Engage in Horse Trading In addition to internally refocusing the resources a unit already controls, tipping point leaders skillfully trade resources they don't need for those of others that they do need. Consider again the case of Bratton. The chiefs of public sector organizations know that the size of their budgets and the number of people they control are often hotly debated because public sector resources are notoriously limited. This makes chiefs of public sector organizations unwilling to advertise excess resources, let alone release them for use by other parts of the larger organization, because that would risk a loss of control over those resources. One result is that over time, some organizations become well endowed with resources they don't need even while they are short of ones they do need. On taking over as chief of the New York Transit Police in 1990, Bratton's general counsel and policy adviser, Dean Esserman (now police chief of Providence, Rhode Island), played a key horse trading role. Esserman discovered that the Transit unit, which was starved for office space, had been running a fleet of unmarked cars in excess of its needs. The New York Division of Parole, on the other hand, was short of cars but had excess office space. Esserman and Bratton offered the obvious trade, which was gratefully accepted by the parole officials. For their part, Transit unit officers were delighted to get the first floor of a prime downtown building. The deal stoked Bratton's credibility within the organization, something that later made it easier for him to introduce more fundamental changes. At the same time, it marked him to his political bosses as a man who could solve problems. Figure 7-2 illustrates how radically Bratton refocused the Transit Police department's resources to break out of the red ocean and execute its blue ocean strategy. The vertical axis here shows the relative level of resource allocation, and the horizontal axis shows the various elements of strategy in which the investments were made. By deemphasizing or virtually eliminating some traditional features of transit police work while increasing emphasis on the others or creating new ones, Bratton achieved a dramatic shift in resource allocation. Whereas the actions of eliminating and reducing cut the costs for the organization, raising certain elements or creating new ones required added investments. As you can see on the strategy canvas, however, the overall investment of resources remained more or less constant. At the same time, the value to citizens went way up. Eliminating the practice of widespread coverage of the subway system and replacing it with a targeted strategy on hot spots enabled the transit police to combat subway crimes more efficiently and effectively. Reducing the involvement of officers in processing arrests or cold spots and creating bust buses significantly raised the value of the police force by allowing officers to concentrate their time and attention on policing the subway. Raising the level of investment in combating quality-of-life crimes rather than big crimes refocused the police resources on crimes that presented constant dangers to citizens' daily lives. Through these moves, the New York Transit Police significantly enhanced the performance of its officers, who were now freed from administrative hassles and assigned clear duties as to what kinds of crimes they should focus on and where to combat them. Are you allocating resources based on old assumptions, or do you seek out and concentrate resources on hot spots? Where are your hot spots? What activities have the greatest performance impact but are resource starved? Where are your cold spots? What activities are resource oversupplied but have scant performance impact? Do you have a horse trader, and what can you trade? Jump the Motivational Hurdle To reach your organization's tipping point and execute blue ocean strategy, you must alert employees to the need for a strategic shift and identify how it can be achieved with limited resources. For a new strategy to become a movement, people must not only recognize what needs to be done, but they must also act on that insight in a sustained and meaningful way. How can you motivate the mass of employees fast and at low cost? When most business leaders want to break from the status quo and transform their organizations, they issue grand strategic visions and turn to massive top-down mobilization initiatives. They act on the assumption that to create massive reactions, proportionate massive actions are required. But this is often a cumbersome, expensive, and time-consuming process, given the wide variety of motivational needs in most large companies. And overarching strategic visions often inspire lip service instead of the intended action. It would be easier to turn an aircraft carrier around in a bathtub. Or is there another way? Instead of diffusing change efforts widely, tipping point leaders follow a reverse course and seek massive concentration. They focus on three factors of disproportionate influence in motivating employees, what we call kingpins, fishbowl management, and atomization. For strategic change to have real impact, employees at every level must move en masse. To trigger an epidemic movement of positive energy, however, you should not spread your efforts thin. Rather, you should concentrate your efforts on kingpins, the key influencers in the organization. These are people inside the organization who are natural leaders, who are well respected and persuasive, or who have an ability to unlock or block access to key resources. As with kingpins in bowling, when you hit them straight on, all the other pins come toppling down. This frees an organization from tackling everyone, and yet in the end everyone is touched and changed. And because in most organizations there are a relatively small number of key influencers, who tend to share common problems and concerns, it is relatively easy for the CEO to identify and motivate them. At the NYPD, for example, Bratton zoomed in on the seventy-six precinct heads as his key influencers and kingpins. Why? Each precinct head directly controlled two hundred to four hundred police officers. Hence, galvanizing these seventy-six heads would have the natural ripple effect of touching and motivating the thirty-sixthousand-deep police force to embrace the new policing strategy. Place Kingpins in a Fishbowl At the heart of motivating the kingpins in a sustained and meaningful way is to shine a spotlight on their actions in a repeated and highly visible way. This is what we refer to as fishbowl management, where kingpins' actions and inaction are made as transparent to others as are fish in a bowl of water. By placing kingpins in a fishbowl in this way you greatly raise the stakes of inaction. Light is shined on who is lagging behind, and a fair stage is set for rapid change agents to shine. For fishbowl management to work it must be based on transparency, inclusion, and fair process.

CHAPTER ELEVEN

Build Execution into Strategy

ACOM PANY I S NOT ON LY TOP MANAG E M E NT, nor is it only middle management. A company is everyone from the top to the front lines. And it is only when all the members of an organization are aligned around a strategy and support it, for better or for worse, that a company stands apart as a great and consistent executor. Overcoming the organizational hurdles to strategy execution is an important step toward that end. It removes the roadblocks that can put a halt to even the best of strategies. But in the end, a company needs to invoke the most fundamental base of action: the attitudes and behavior of its people deep in the organization. You must create a culture of trust and commitment that motivates people to execute the agreed strategy—not to the letter, but to the spirit. People's minds and hearts must align with the new strategy so that at the level of the individual, people embrace it of their own accord and willingly go beyond compulsory execution to voluntary cooperation in carrying it out. Where blue ocean strategy is concerned, this challenge is heightened. Trepidation builds as people are required to step out of their comfort zones and change how they have worked in the past. They wonder, What are the real reasons for this change? Is top management honest when it speaks of building future growth through a change in strategic course? Or are they trying to make us redundant and work us out of our jobs? The more removed people are from the top and the less they have been involved in the creation of the strategy, the more this trepidation builds. On the front line, at the very level at which a strategy must be executed day in and day out, people can resent having a strategy thrust upon them with little regard for what they think and feel. Just when you think you have done everything right, things can suddenly go very wrong in your front line. This brings us to the sixth principle of blue ocean strategy: To build people's trust and commitment deep in the ranks and inspire their voluntary cooperation, companies need to build execution into strategy from the start. That principle allows companies to minimize the management risk of distrust, noncooperation, and even sabotage. This management risk is relevant to strategy execution in both red and blue oceans, but it is greater for blue ocean strategy because its execution often requires significant change. Hence, minimizing such risk is essential as companies execute blue ocean strategy. Companies must reach beyond the usual suspects of carrots and sticks. They must reach to fair process in the making and executing of strategy. Our research shows that fair process is a key variable that distinguishes successful blue ocean strategic moves from those that failed. The presence or absence of fair process can make or break a company's best execution efforts. Poor Process Can Ruin Strategy Execution Consider the experience of a global leader in supplying waterbased liquid coolants for metalworking industries. We'll call this organization Lubber. Because of the many processing parameters in metal-based manufacturing, there are several hundred complex types of coolants to choose from. Choosing the right coolant is a delicate process. Products must first be tested on production machines before purchasing, and the decision often rests on fuzzy logic. The result is machine downtime and sampling costs, and these are expensive for customers and Lubber alike. To offer customers a leap in value, Lubber devised a strategy to eliminate the complexity and costs of the trial phase. Using artificial intelligence, it developed an expert system that cut the failure rate in selecting coolants to less than 10 percent from an industry average of 50 percent. The system also reduced machine downtime, eased coolant management, and raised the overall quality of work pieces produced. As for Lubber, the sales process was dramatically simplified, giving sales representatives more time to gain new sales and dropping the costs per sale. This win-win value innovation strategic move, however, was doomed from the start. It wasn't that the strategy was not good or that the expert system did not work; it worked exceptionally well. The strategy was doomed because the sales force fought it. Having not been engaged in the strategy-making process nor apprised of the rationale for the strategic shift, sales reps saw the expert system in a light no one on the design team or management team had ever imagined. To them, it was a direct threat to what they saw as their most valuable contribution—tinkering in the trial phase to find the right water-based coolant from the long list of possible candidates. All the wonderful benefits—having a way to avoid the hassle-filled part of their job, having more time to pull in more sales, and winning more contracts by standing out in the industry—went unappreciated. With the sales force feeling threatened and often working against the expert system by expressing doubts about its effectiveness to customers, sales did not take off. After cursing its hubris and learning the hard way the importance of dealing with managerial risk up front based on the proper process, management was forced to pull the expert system from the market and work on rebuilding trust with its sales representatives. What, then, is fair process? And how does it allow companies to build execution into strategy? The theme of fairness or justice has preoccupied writers and philosophers throughout the ages. But the direct theoretical origin of fair process traces back to two social scientists: John W. Thibaut and Laurens Walker. In the mid-1970s, they combined their interest in the psychology of justice with the study of process, creating the term procedural justice. 1 Focusing their attention on legal settings, they sought to understand what makes people trust a legal system so that they will comply with laws without being coerced. Their research established that people care as much about the justice of the process through which an outcome is produced as they do about the outcome itself. People's satisfaction with the outcome and their commitment to it rose when procedural justice was exercised.2 Fair process is our managerial expression of procedural justice theory. As in legal settings, fair process builds execution into strategy by creating people's buy-in up front. When fair process is exercised in the strategy-making process, people trust that a level playing field exists. This inspires them to cooperate voluntarily in executing the resulting strategic decisions. Voluntary cooperation is more than mechanical execution, where people do only what it takes to get by. It involves going beyond the call of duty, wherein individuals exert energy and initiative to the best of their abilities—even subordinating personal self-interest— to execute resulting strategies.3 Figure 8-1 presents the causal flow we observed among fair process, attitudes, and behavior. The Three E Principles of Fair Process There are three mutually reinforcing elements that define fair process: engagement, explanation, and clarity of expectation. Whether people are senior executives or shop floor employees, they all look to these elements. We call them the three E principles of fair process. Engagement means involving individuals in the strategic decisions that affect them by asking for their input and allowing them to refute the merits of one another's ideas and assumptions. Engagement communicates management's respect for individuals and their ideas. Encouraging refutation sharpens everyone's thinking and builds better collective wisdom. Engagement results in better strategic decisions by management and greater commitment from all involved to execute those decisions. Explanation means that everyone involved and affected should understand why final strategic decisions are made as they are. An explanation of the thinking that underlies decisions makes people confident that managers have considered their opinions and have made decisions impartially in the overall interests of the company. An explanation allows employees to trust managers' intentions even if their own ideas have been rejected. It also serves as a powerful feedback loop that enhances learning. Expectation clarity requires that after a strategy is set, managers state clearly the new rules of the game. Although the expectations may be demanding, employees should know up front what standards they will be judged by and the penalties for failure. What are the goals of the new strategy? What are the new targets and milestones? Who is responsible for what? To achieve fair process, it matters less what the new goals, expectations, and responsibilities are and more that they are clearly understood. When people clearly understand what is expected of them, political jockeying and favoritism are minimized, and people can focus on executing the strategy rapidly. Taken together, these three criteria collectively lead to judgments of fair process. This is important, because any subset of the three does not create judgments of fair process. A Tale of Two Plants How do the three E principles of fair process work to affect strategy execution deep in an organization? Consider the experience of an elevator systems manufacturer we'll call Elco. In the late 1980s, sales in the elevator industry declined. Excess office space left some large U.S. cities with vacancy rates as high as 20 percent. With domestic demand falling, Elco set out to offer buyers a leap in value while lowering its costs to stimulate new demand and break from the competition. In its quest to create and execute a blue ocean strategy, the company realized that it needed to replace its batch-manufacturing system with a cellular approach that would allow self-directed teams to achieve superior performance. The management team was in agreement and ready to go. To execute this key element of its strategy, the team adopted what looked like the fastest and smartest way to move forward. It would first install the new system at Elco's Chester plant and then roll it out to its second plant, High Park. The logic was simple. The Chester plant had exemplary employee relations, so much so that the workers had decertified their own union. Management was certain it could count on employee cooperation to execute the strategic shift in manufacturing. In the company's words, "They were the ideal work force." Next, Elco would roll out the process to its plant in High Park, where a strong union was expected to resist that, or any other, change. Management was counting on having achieved a degree of momentum for execution at Chester that it hoped would have positive spillover effects on High Park. The theory was good. In practice, however, things took an unpredicted turn. The introduction of the new manufacturing process at the Chester plant quickly led to disorder and rebellion. Within a few months, both cost and quality performance were in free fall. Employees were talking about bringing back the union. Having lost control, the despairing plant manager called Elco's industrial psychologist for help. In contrast, the High Park plant, despite its reputation for resistance, had accepted the strategic shift in the manufacturing process. Every day, the High Park manager waited for the anticipated meltdown, but it never came. Even when people didn't like the decisions, they felt they had been treated fairly, and so they willingly participated in the rapid execution of the new manufacturing process, a pivotal component of the company's new strategy. A closer look at the way the strategic shift was made at the two plants reveals the reasons behind this apparent anomaly. At the Chester plant, Elco managers violated all three of the basic principles of fair process. First, they failed to engage employees in the strategic decisions that directly affected them. Lacking expertise in cellular manufacturing, Elco brought in a consulting firm to design a master plan for the conversion. The consultants were briefed to work quickly and with minimal disturbance to employees so that fast, painless implementation could be achieved. The consultants followed the instructions. When Chester employees arrived at work they discovered strangers at the plant who not only dressed differently—wearing dark suits, white shirts, and ties—but also spoke in low tones to one another. To minimize disturbance, they didn't interact with employees. Instead they quietly hovered behind people's backs, taking notes and drawing diagrams. The rumor circulated that after employees went home in the afternoon, these same people would swarm across the plant floor, snoop around people's workstations, and have heated discussions. During this period, the plant manager was increasingly absent. He was spending more time at Elco's head office in meetings with the consultants—sessions deliberately scheduled away from the plant so as not to distract the employees. But the plant manager's absence produced the opposite effect. As people grew anxious, wondering why the captain of their ship seemed to be deserting them, the rumor mill moved into high gear. Everyone became convinced that the consultants would downsize the plant. They were sure they were about to lose their jobs. The fact that the plant manager was always gone without any explanation—obviously, he was avoiding them—could only mean that management was, they thought, "trying to put one over on us." Trust and commitment at the Chester plant deteriorated quickly. Soon, people were bringing in newspaper clippings about other plants around the country that had been shut down with the help of consultants. Employees saw themselves as imminent victims of management's hidden intention to downsize and work people out of their jobs. In fact, Elco managers had no intention of closing the plant. They wanted to cut waste, freeing people to produce higher-quality elevators faster at lower cost to leapfrog the competition. But plant employees could not have known that. Managers at Chester also didn't explain why strategic decisions were being made the way they were and what those decisions meant to employees' careers and work methods. Management unveiled the master plan for change in a thirty-minute session with employees. The audience heard that their time-honored way of working would be abolished and replaced by something called "cellular manufacturing." No one explained why the strategic shift was needed, how the company needed to break away from the competition to stimulate new demand, and why the shift in the manufacturing process was a key element of that strategy. Employees sat in stunned silence, with no understanding of the rationale behind the change. The managers mistook this for acceptance, forgetting how long it had taken them over the preceding few months to get comfortable with the idea of shifting to cellular manufacturing to execute the new strategy. Master plan in hand, management quickly began rearranging the plant. When employees asked what the new layout aimed to achieve, the response was "efficiency gains." The managers didn't have time to explain why efficiency had to be improved and didn't want to worry employees. But lacking an intellectual understanding of what was happening to them, some employees began feeling sick as they came to work. Managers also neglected to make clear what would be expected of employees under the new manufacturing process. They informed employees that they would no longer be judged on individual performance but rather on the performance of the cell. They said that faster or more experienced employees would have to pick up the slack for slower or less experienced colleagues. But they didn't elaborate. How the new cellular system was supposed to work, managers didn't make clear. Violations of the principles of fair process undermined employees' trust in the strategic shift and in management. In fact, the new cell design offered tremendous benefits to employees—for example, making vacations easier to schedule and giving them the opportunity to broaden their skills and engage in a greater variety of work. Yet employees could see only its negative side. They began taking out their fear and anger on one another. Fights erupted on the plant floor as employees refused to help those they called "lazy people who can't finish their own jobs" or interpreted offers of help as meddling, responding with, "This is my job. You keep to your own workstation."Chester's model work force was falling apart. For the first time in the plant manager's career, employees refused to do as they were asked, turning down assignments "even if you fire me." They felt they could no longer trust the once popular plant manager, so they began to go around him, taking their complaints directly to his boss at the head office. In the absence of fair process, the Chester plant's employees rejected the transformation and refused to play their role in executing the new strategy. In contrast, management at the High Park plant abided by all three principles of fair process when introducing the strategic shift. When the consultants came to the plant, the plant manager introduced them to all employees. Management engaged employees by holding a series of plantwide meetings, where corporate executives openly discussed the declining business conditions and the company's need for a change in strategic course to break from the competition and simultaneously achieve higher value at lower cost. They explained that they had visited other companies' plants and had seen the productivity improvements that cellular manufacturing could bring. They explained how this would be a pivotal determinant of the company's ability to achieve its new strategy. They announced a proaction-time policy to calm employees' justifiable fears of layoffs. As old performance measures were discarded, managers worked with employees to develop new ones and to establish each cell team's new responsibilities. Goals and expectations were made clear to employees. By practicing the three principles of fair process in tandem, management won the understanding and support of High Park employees. The employees spoke of their plant manager with admiration, and they commiserated with the difficulties Elco's managers had in executing the new strategy and making the changeover to cellular manufacturing. They concluded that it had been a necessary, worthwhile, and positive experience. Elco's managers still regard this experience as one of the most painful in their careers.

They learned that people in the front line care as much about the proper process as those at the top. By violating fair process in making and rolling out strategies, managers can turn their best employees into their worst, earning their distrust of and resistance to the very strategy they depend on them to execute. But if managers practice fair process, the worst employees can turn into the best and can execute even difficult strategic shifts with their willing commitment while building their trust. Why Does Fair Process Matter? Why is fair process important in shaping people's attitudes and behavior? Specifically, why does the observance or violation of fair process in strategy making have the power to make or break a strategy's execution? It all comes down to intellectual and emotional recognition. Emotionally, individuals seek recognition of their value, not as "labor," "personnel," or "human resources" but as human beings who are treated with full respect and dignity and appreciated for their individual worth regardless of hierarchical level. Intellectually, individuals seek recognition that their ideas are sought after and given thoughtful reflection, and that others think enough of their intelligence to explain their thinking to them. Such frequently cited expressions in our interviews as "that goes for everyone I know" or "every person wants to feel" and constant references to "people" and "human beings" reinforce the point that managers must see the nearly universal value of the intellectual and emotional recognition that fair process conveys. Intellectual and Emotional Recognition Theory Using fair process in strategy making is strongly linked to both intellectual and emotional recognition. It proves through action that there is an eagerness to trust and cherish the individual as well as a deep-seated confidence in the individual's knowledge, talents, and expertise. When individuals feel recognized for their intellectual worth, they are willing to share their knowledge; in fact, they feel inspired to impress and confirm the expectation of their intellectual value, suggesting active ideas and knowledge sharing. Similarly, when individuals are treated with emotional recognition, they feel emotionally tied to the strategy and inspired to give their all. Indeed, in Frederick Herzberg's classic study on motivation, recognition was found to inspire strong intrinsic motivation, causing people to go beyond the call of duty and engage in voluntary cooperation.4 Hence, to the extent that fair process judgments convey intellectual and emotional recognition, people will better apply their knowledge and expertise, as well as their voluntary efforts to cooperate for the organization's success in executing strategy. However, there is a flip side to this that is deserving of equal, if not more, attention: the violation of fair process and, with it, the violation of recognizing individuals' intellectual and emotional worth. The observed pattern of thought and behavior can be summarized as follows. If individuals are not treated as though their knowledge is valued, they will feel intellectual indignation and will not share their ideas and expertise; rather, they will hoard their best thinking and creative ideas, preventing new insights from seeing the light of day. What's more, they will reject others' intellectual worth as well. It's as if they were saying, "You don't value my ideas. So I don't value your ideas, nor do I trust in or care about the strategic decisions you've reached." Similarly, to the extent that people's emotional worth is not recognized, they will feel angry and will not invest their energy in their actions; rather, they will drag their feet and apply counterefforts, including sabotage, as in the case of Elco's Chester plant. This often leads employees to push for rolling back strategies that have been imposed unfairly, even when the strategies themselves were good ones—critical to the company's success or beneficial to employees and managers themselves. Lacking trust in the strategymaking process, people lack trust in the resulting strategies. Such is the emotional power that fair process can provoke. Figure 8-2 shows the observed causal pattern. Fair Process and Blue Ocean Strategy Commitment, trust, and voluntary cooperation are not merely attitudes or behaviors. They are intangible capital. When people have trust, they have heightened confidence in one another's intentions and actions. When they have commitment, they are even willing to override personal self-interest in the interests of the company. If you ask any company that has created and successfully executed a blue ocean strategy, managers will be quick to rattle off how important this intangible capital is to their success. Similarly, managers from companies that have failed in executing blue ocean strategies will point out that the lack of this capital contributed to their failure. These companies were not able to orchestrate strategic shifts because they lacked people's trust and commitment. Commitment, trust, and voluntary cooperation allow companies to stand apart in the speed, quality, and consistency of their execution and to implement strategic shifts fast at low cost. The question companies wrestle with is how to create trust, commitment, and voluntary cooperation deep in the organization. You don't do it by separating strategy formulation from execution. Although this disconnect may be a hallmark of most companies' practice, it is also a hallmark of slow and questionable implementation, and mechanical follow-through at best. Of course, traditional incentives of power and money—carrots and sticks—help. But they fall short of inspiring human behavior that goes beyond outcomedriven self-interest. Where behavior cannot be monitored with certainty, there is still plenty of room for foot-dragging and sabotage. The exercise of fair process gets around this dilemma. By organizing the strategy formulation process around the principles of fair process, you can build execution into strategy making from the start. With fair process, people tend to be committed to support the resulting strategy even when it is viewed as not favorable or at odds with their perception of what is strategically correct for their unit. People realize that compromises and sacrifices are necessary in building a strong company. They accept the need for short-term personal sacrifices in order to advance the long-term interests of the corporation. This acceptance is conditional, however, on the presence of fair process. Whatever the context in which a company's blue ocean strategy is executed—be it working with a joint venture partner to outsource component manufacturing, reorienting the sales force, transforming the manufacturing process, relocating a company's call center from the United States to India—we have consistently observed this dynamic at work.